Juno's Journey

Loosely based on true events.

A W Marshall

Juno's Journey

INTRODUCTION

On the 7th of March 2022, my beloved rescue lurcher, Juno, went missing when she was being looked after by a dog sitter.

My partner and I were both working a lot at the time and had recently moved house, so we needed to get a regular dog walker and dog sitter that we could rely on and trust to look after her.

So, we hired someone who we thought could be trustworthy and just starting out their business. We thought we'd be decent people and help them out. After all, everyone deserves a chance and must start from somewhere. Besides, being a friend of a friend – we believed we could put our trust in them.

Little did we know what was about to happen… or how it was going to end.

This book is based loosely on a true account of what happened to our beloved dog for the 10 days she was missing, the unimaginable horror I experienced during this time, and the unconditional love and support we received from our local community and beyond – which, ultimately, saved her life.

We even featured on a local tv program which covered briefly the incident a few months after it had happened.

My incredible dog survived all the odds, and it really is a miracle she is alive today.

This is her story.

CONTENTS

Juno's Journey

ACKNOWLEDGMENTS

I would like to dedicate and thank every single one of you who has supported Juno in her recovery, by donating and who has followed her journey. Thank you to the vets that helped give Juno another chance at life, and a great big thank you to the workmen who found Juno just in time.

Juno's Journey

DAY 1 – MONDAY 7TH MARCH 2022.

My dog Juno was at the dog sitters, as both my partner and I were at work for long periods of time, and she suffered from separation anxiety so couldn't be left for long on her own. I was imagining all the fun she would be having, playing with all the other dogs and letting off copious amounts of steam.

At around 6:30pm, I received a text from my partner to let me know she was back home from work. She said that Juno wasn't at the house. 'When's the dog sitter bringing Juno back?' he asked. 'It's getting quite late now.'

I was at work currently – as a healthcare assistant working on an NHS covid ward, I was in the middle of a long and draining 12.5 – hour shift – so I was too busy to reply to her, but Juno should have been back by 4pm.

She then asked, 'Do they still have Juno?'

Before I had a chance to reply, I received another text – the worst kind of news you could ever receive as a dog owner: 'Juno has escaped from their garden, she's gone missing! They say they are looking everywhere for her and got everyone out looking for her. I'm going to call all the local shelters and kennels.'

As I received this message while I was still at work, and although I was franticly sick with worry, I had to stay cool, calm, and collected and finish the rest of the shift at least. I had many emotions and thoughts racing through my mind – panic, fear, and anger being the main ones – but I was just trying not to think about it all too much. I tried ever so hard to stay professional and hold it together for the remaining time of my shift.

After all, dogs go missing all the time, and – most of the time – they're found within a few hours or days, aren't they?

When I had finally finished work, I eventually got round to replying to the texts, asking, 'What time did the dog sitter say she escaped?'

My partner replied, 'Not long ago.'

The time was now 7:30pm, and the dog sitter had previously agreed to drop Juno off at around 4 in the afternoon, so how had she just recently escaped? Why hadn't they dropped her off when they were meant to? Had she escaped earlier, and if so, why didn't the dog sitter call or message me, like any other professional dog sitter would do?

I remember looking at their professional page online at around lunch time on my break briefly to check of any updates and to see if she was having a good time there – I noticed Juno wasn't in any of the photo's – but I thought at that time maybe the dog sitter gave Juno a rest and was being looked after at their residence by an acquaintance whilst out walking other dogs.

My partner called the police to inform them, but they just said they couldn't assist with lost dogs.

Trying to piece everything together and reassure myself that everything was going to be OK, I replied, 'She may come back to the garden or our house.' I also told her, 'My childhood dog ran away on a walk once, and we were looking everywhere frantically. In the end, he was waiting for us at the fence where he'd run away from. Hopefully Juno will do the same.' I then told my partner to call around our old neighbourhood to see if Juno might have gone back to our old house, having recently moved.

After finally leaving the hospital after a long and grueling shift, I made my way hastily to my car. I could feel my chest tightening and my breathing becoming shallower as I walked. Then I had to sit through and endure what felt like the longest drive home of my life; I listened to loud music the whole way – mostly heavy metal and a bit of Skrillex – trying to distract myself from the dreadful news I'd received.

I eventually got home at around 9pm.

That night, I couldn't eat; I couldn't think straight. The image of Juno lying outside somewhere in the cold, all alone, in the dark... I just couldn't face it – especially as I know she suffers from separation anxiety, having been a lockdown puppy before we rescued her.

All kinds of questions were running around through my mind: Where could she be? What if someone had stolen her? What if she'd been killed? I just felt so hopeless and much rage at the dog sitter – and so much confusion and mixed emotions.

"Tell me what the dog sitter told you," I said to my partner, wanting to wrap my head around what had happened.

She told me that someone had left the dog sitter's back gate open and that both of their dogs and Juno had escaped, but that only their dogs had come back.

I immediately gathered Juno's lead and harness, my other dog (who hadn't gone to the dog sitters, as he didn't need as many walks and as much stimulation as Juno), and some treats, then my partner and I jumped straight into the car to go out looking for her. We drove down to the park we would always take her to when we lived at our old house, hoping we would find her there.

After around 30 minutes or so spent searching and calling her name in the dark around the park - with no signs of her to be seen or heard – we got back into the car and drove around our old neighbourhood – but still, there were no signs. We were frantically panicking, what if we find her dead?

So, reluctantly, we headed back home for the night, hoping that if she was still in the area, she would pick up our scent, or try to make her own way home.

As my partner had been waiting for me to get back home from work, she told me she had contacted as many online missing dog groups (both local and nationwide) as possible. We hoped one of these would help bring Juno back to us.

I couldn't sleep at all that night, constantly worried sick of where Juno could be.

DAY 2 – TUESDAY 8TH MARCH 2022.

Luckily, I didn't have work today, but this gave me more time to stress about Juno going missing.

At around 11:30am, I received a text from my partner – who was at work – to say that an admin from one the missing dog groups was waiting for me to get in contact with them. My partner then added me to the online group chat.

Shortly after, the admin asked me for some information about Juno and a photo of her, so that they could create an online missing poster to help spread the word. 'She's a black lurcher-type dog and has a heart-shaped white patch on her chest.'

They replied, 'Thank you,' once I'd sent them everything they needed, 'I'll get the poster done in the next 15 minutes and post the link on the main page; our team will share it so it will hopefully get many shares. Ask the dog sitter if they can make sure Juno has access to the garden.'

The admin also told us in the group chat: 'If possible, please ask the dog sitter to hang up an item of theirs in the garden – such as a worn but not yet washed piece of clothing or bedding. It helps keep and attract the dog there if they do come back, especially if no one is at home.'

At least we knew now that we had more eyes out searching for her, - thanks to the great invention of the internet and social media – and that – hopefully – she would be found.

I then got alerted about a post someone had shared on a local online page, of a black lurcher spotted on the railway line. My heart sank and pounded, I immediately added that person on the online platform and quickly sent them a message, asking what they had seen and where. I also sent them over a photo of Juno for reference.

According to the online platform, the post had been made around 1pm on the day Juno went missing – hours before she had supposedly run out of the dog sitters' garden.

At this point, I sent a text to my partner to suggest that I felt the dog sitter had been lying about what had happened and wasn't telling the whole truth. I also wasn't sure why the dog sitter had apparently added my partner on their personal profile on the online platform and not me, when I was usually the main one contacting them in regard to Juno.

It was at that moment I remembered that I was looking at their dog walking and sitting page and not seeing Juno in any of the photos after the first walk that day. I tried not to think about it too much now as we didn't know what had exactly happened. All we could do was hope she is ok.

I then told the missing dogs group admin that I'd just been in contact with a person who may have possibly seen her on the railway line and had taken a photo of her, and they then suggested I alert the staff at the local national railway company, which I did; they reported that they hadn't seen anything, but that they would keep an eye out.

The dog sitter was starting to act peculiarly in general.

For one thing, they weren't replying to any of my messages, which I was starting to find extremely strange; if I'd personally lost someone's dog, I'd be frantic, I wouldn't stop thinking about it and go straight over to the owners' house - after contacting them to tell them what had happened – and help them search for their dog until it was found safe. I certainly wouldn't be ignoring them! I then double checked their online business page where they posted the dog walks from yesterday, and the dog walk they posted at around 12pm – but Juno wasn't in any of the photos, just in the photos of the morning walk. So, she must have got lost around that time – after 12pm!

My partner soon replied to my text, agreeing with me. 'I had a feeling they were only giving me a half-truth,' she said.

By now, I was feeling betrayed, conned, and super angry.

Something didn't feel right.

'I don't think they did anything bad,' my partner continued, 'I just think they panicked, and realised that they couldn't find her. I think they're embarrassed. But it will be on their head if anything was to happen to her.'

'Yeah,' I replied, 'it will.'

Just then, the person who had spotted the lurcher on the railway replied to my message stating that it must have been her! Saying it was at a distance but that the photo and what they saw looked just like each other. They had said Juno was spotted heading northwest of the railway, wouldn't come to them when called to try and get her attention – which was extremely unlike her – and then they said they will help keep a look out for me in case they see anything.

'Aww thank you,' I gratefully replied. 'I just hope she doesn't end up going onto any farms and get shot.'

I do disagree to the fact that farmers are allowed to shoot dogs that enter their land – even if it's a public right of way or not, - and kill the dogs even if they haven't caused any deaths to their livestock.

Then the person who had spotted Juno on the railway reassured me that she would be OK and bets the dog sitter feels awful.

'Yeah, she's only 20 months old; not even two years old yet. And yes, I hope they feel awful – they didn't tell us until the evening that she was missing!'

They cursed in shock and agreed that the dog sitter should've told me straight away, they then asked where she went missing from.

I completely agreed with them. After all, if I was in this situation – where I'd lost someone's dog that I personally was looking after – I'd be phoning the owners straight away! And I'd be in constant contact and would be out there looking every day and night, offering my help!

I replied then as to where I guessed she had escaped from as I didn't quite know where the dog sitter's main residence was, only that they said they lived near a garage.

I quickly replied, 'thank you!' and I had a good idea where to go looking for her now.

They then wished me luck on finding her and said will let me know if they find anything. I was going to head down that way with my other dog later today.

I messaged my partner – who was still at work – telling her what the person had said, and soon I got my other dog ready to go and look for her. I was annoyed at myself that we hadn't gone looking that way last night, but of course, we hadn't heard about this sighting then.

My partner agreed it would be a good idea to follow the tracks of the railway line, so that's what I did. I went out searching for a good hour or so, but as I couldn't find her anywhere or hear anything that could lead me to her, I then headed back to the house.

At around 3pm I texted my partner: 'No luck. But taking our other dog out and about hopefully would leave some familiar scents and hopefully that would be enough to attract her.'

At 5pm, my partner then replied: 'Hopefully… it's not looking good.'

Still angry at the person who was supposed to have been taking care of my dog, I sent my partner another message: 'No apologies from the dog sitter either.'

My partner agreed. 'Yeah, they've been unusually quiet for someone who did something wrong, even if it was a simple mistake. Not helping at all.'

'Maybe we should call our old neighbour and make sure that they haven't seen anything,' I suggested, 'and ask their opinion on what we should do. As technically, we could get the dog sitter done – they're not even insured yet!'

She replied, 'If she's gone forever then yeah, we have to do something.'

I didn't, of course, want to think about that potential outcome.

After no direct contact from the dog sitter, I decided to message them on their online business page, asking, 'Any sign of Juno?'

They just simply replied, 'No nothing' – and that was it. For someone who was supposed to be looking after someone else's dog and a dog lover themselves, they sure didn't seem like they cared much at all.

I wanted to get their side of the story, even it was their job to tell me, so – at around 11:30pm that night, I asked, 'So what actually happened?'

Their reply came a few moments later: 'I let her out in the garden with my dogs, but she leapt the fence. I tried to follow where she went but couldn't keep up with her. I thought she may have gone straight to yours so that's where I went, but there was no sign of her.'

Leapt the fence? I thought. They had told my partner she had run out of an open gate!... none of this seemed to be adding up.

Taking a large, deep breath in, and trying not to show much anger or annoyance towards their actions, I replied, 'It's surprising how high she can jump. I wonder why she did it as it's just not like her at all. I've got in contact with someone online who had spotted her down by the railway tracks northwest, but Juno wouldn't come to them. Me and my other dog went all around that area today looking for her, but there was no sign of her.'

They then replied with, 'It's not that high really if you look on the inside of the garden – there is a smaller wall that she leapt off.' They also stated that they thought Juno was missing us as she was whining most of the night, which isn't like her at all.

'Ah I see,' I replied. 'Yeah, probably. So did she go in the direction of our house when she ran away?'

They said, 'Yes.' Then went on to say they had asked around if anyone had seen a black lurcher come past this way and someone had said the local train station, so the dog sitter said they made their way over but there was no sign so decided to check back at our house.

'This is so out of character for her,' I replied. 'Although, in our garden, I don't take her out there unless she has her lead on – we're waiting to get proper fences in place.'

They then said that Juno doesn't usually need a lead on in their garden as she's usually quite content and they would never have expected this to happen.

So, she was usually content when at the dog sitters, and this is very out of character for her – this made me start to think that something must have happened to startle her enough to make her flee.

Was the dog sitter hiding something? Did they hit her? Did their dogs have a scrap with her? All these questions were running through my mind.

I didn't know what to believe or what had really happened, but I was determined to get to the bottom of it.

So, another night without Juno, wondering and imagining where she could possibly be.

Hopefully tomorrow will be a better day.

DAY 3 – WEDNESDAY 9TH MARCH 2022.

At 8am, I messaged the dog sitter again: 'I just hope she is safe and comes back.'

They agreed.

After I'd spent almost another morning worrying about what had happened to Juno, the dog sitter was the one to message me first, at 3:15pm asking if there was any news on her.

'No,' I replied. 'I'm probably going to have to start to prepare for the worst – never seeing her again.'

They then – rather sketching and oddly – came back to me with an apology (which was the actual first time they had apologised to me since she'd gone missing!), then told me they think that she's been picked up by someone and kept by them.

WHAT?!

Now even more confused and hurt, I messaged back, 'What makes you say that?? Anyway, I'll make her too hot to handle, so if someone has got her and is keeping her, everyone around town will see her and know she's not theirs!'

They then just stated that it's because surely, she would have been found by now.

I ended the conversation with, 'I'll start putting up posters around town,' to which they replied with a simple: 'OK.' There were no offers of help with handing out the posters, no saying that they will go out looking for her with us... nothing. It was unfathomable!

Annoyed, upset and angry, I sent a screenshot of our conversation to my partner, and her reply was: 'Yeah, I don't fully trust that let's just see how this plays out. Don't call them suspicious yet. I'll get some more advice from the admin from the missing dogs online group.'

The admin messaged us via the group chat: 'Hi, just checking that there are no new sightings, not seen anything myself.'

My partner sent the message: 'No new sightings as of yet, I'm checking every minute,' to which the admin replied, 'OK, will keep sharing the poster around online and checking other sites, hopefully we get good news soon.'

'I hope so,' said my partner, 'It's getting very hard now, I hope someone finds her soon.'

The admin stated: 'Not unusual to not have sightings for this amount of time, so fingers crossed for something soon.'

I then informed the admin, 'The person who had seen Juno on the railway on Monday afternoon said they'll be looking out for her too, me and my other dog had been all around that particular area and even around in the woodlands but saw nothing.'

'Good idea to be taking the other dog around, she may pick up the scent,' the admin agreed.

At around half 6 that evening, I sent a screenshot of my recent conversation I had with the dog sitter to the admin, to see what they could make of it. 'Does it seem a bit suspicious to you?' I asked, to which he replied, 'Yes, it is, it is a possibility with any missing dog, but it doesn't happen that often.'

I then told the admin I had told the dog sitter I'll be getting some posters printed out and will place them up all around the town and a few other towns further out.

The admin replied, 'Was going to suggest that, will send you a link for free posters now. They don't take long to send out, if you get some poly pockets and put the poster upside down, it will protect it from the rain. Without any evidence that she's been picked up, it's important to keep up with trying to get a sighting. You can also save the poster direct from our group page – just send that file to the printing company.'

'Thank you,' I said. 'I thought of physical posters because the more people who see her, the better – they can pick up on it if they see someone walking her.'

The admin then replied, 'Yes, well worth doing. I am living locally, but if there are and sightings, I am happy to come and help if I can. I have tagged some local volunteers on your post as well.'

A little while later, I informed them that I'd ordered the 50 free posters, hoping they will arrive by tomorrow or Friday.

'OK, that's good, just need to keep the publicity up to get the sightings, still I think she's in the local area.'

'I do hope so,' I replied. 'Do you think I should put posters as far west to the nearest city, and as far east as the next nearest city, and everywhere in between? Or maybe a bit further north too? One of my colleagues said they had told one of their family members who lives not too far away from here, to spread the word.'

The admin replied by suggesting we concentrate on local and surrounding areas for now, as they are doing all they can sharing all around this part of the country and even further.

'I've also messaged Juno's previous dog walker; they are based over the next town from us and used to take Juno out all the time before we moved.'

The admin then stated to keep looking along the valley, 'the town and areas surrounding where Juno's previous dog walker lives is worth doing in case she goes over the top of the next valley.'

'I hope this works,' I said, before adding, 'I've also sent them a digital copy of the missing poster for them to also share around. They even said that it's not like Juno to run away like she did.'

The admin then said, 'Well worth making sure they know. Depends on what caused her to run off, have you had a look around the area she went missing for any CCTV?'

'The dog sitter seems to think that Juno was missing us and looking for us, but she's been staying there for quite a few times previously and has been fine, they even said she's usually so content,' I explained. 'I will look around to see if there is any CCTV.'

'Hard to tell, but it is possible,' they replied. 'She doesn't know your home very well at the moment, does she?'

'We moved a few months ago, but we've also looked around our old neighbourhood in case she was there, and nothing.'

'OK, make sure a couple of posters are in that area too, close to your old house.'

'Will do,' I replied, 'thanks.'

Earlier, as I had told the admin, I had sent a message to Juno's previous dog walker: 'Hi, would you be able to do me a big favour please? Juno has gone missing; please could you keep an eye out on your walks and spread the word if anyone has seen a black lurcher?'

Quickly replying back: 'Aww no!! I hope you're OK. When and where did it happen? I will spread the word. Have you done a post or anything online?'

I replied: 'She escaped from the dog sitter in the local area, she was last seen on Monday afternoon by the local railway line. I've got a digital poster I can send you the link to. Thank you. Just hoping she's safe.' I proceeded to send the link online.

They then asked: 'Did she run off from a walk? She's usually good so something must have startled her. Who was she with, if you don't mind me asking?'

I then told them who the dog sitter was, and that Juno had escaped from the garden, to which they replied, 'Right, I'll keep an eye out on the local groups and such. I know who you are on about, will keep a keen eye out for her. Hope she's OK – and you are too.'

My heart dropped to the pit of my stomach when they said they knew who the dog sitter was. Had they done something similar previously?

'Thank you,' I said. 'I'm just so shocked, it's not like her at all. And it's odd how the person who took the photo of Juno at the railway said she wouldn't even come to them – she usually comes to anyone and everyone, she loves people.' I had then sent the old dog walker the post.

'Something must have happened then, I'm guessing.'

'I really hope she's OK,' I continued. 'Me and my other dog went around looking along following the railway path and a bit further, but there was no sign of anything. I hope she will pick up our scent.'

Juno's previous dog walker then told me that they'll be over this way on Friday so will happily go and look after one of their walks.

'Thank you,' I said, 'I hope she's not gone too far. One of my friends said to maybe knock on peoples' doors around the area. Do you think that would be a good idea to do?' I asked.

'Most definitely. Especially if she's escaped locally. Does she have any favourite places you guys go walking at all?'

'Just the local park really. We did go there on Monday night, but she wasn't anywhere to be found.'

'She could've been hiding or something,' they suggested. 'Go back every night and check.'

I told them that I would do that. They then said, 'Dogs are creatures of habit. Hopefully she'll go somewhere familiar. I'll keep an eye out. So sorry about your situation, fingers crossed she'll be OK. Has anyone been out with a drone or something, or a trap? There are people you can contact.'

I hadn't thought of that, I didn't even know things like that even existed as I had never been through this situation before. 'No, they haven't, I replied, 'how would I go about it?'

They then informed me about an online group dedicated to using drones to search for lost dogs – a group of people who are professional and some hobbyists who help people find their missing dogs using specialist drone technology – and suggested I post about Juno on doglost.co.uk.

'Try these as well, they said, 'they've helped a few of my clients who have had missing dogs – all been found too.'

I thanked them and went straight to look up the drone group online. I soon sent their admin a message, explaining what I needed but as this was the first time doing this, I wasn't sure how to go about it.

At just past 8 in the evening they replied: 'OK, you need to put up a post on the main group and give a full postcode of where the dog went missing from – or the what3words if you have it – and as much information as possible.'

So, with this new potential avenue of help, I got to work and then went straight to bed for the night in hopes of some good news tomorrow.

DAY 4 – THURSDAY 10TH MARCH 2022.

At 1pm, I sent a text message to my partner – as she was at work again: 'I just looked around the park once again where we went the first night and still no sign of her there,' to which she replied,

'Where on earth is she?'

'I wonder if the dog sitter knows she got picked up and knows the person who has her,' I said in a message, thinking out loud. 'I've contacted the pub the dog sitter commonly uses, and they said we can put a poster up there when we get some physical copies.'

My partner replied, 'Yeah, we will watch them closely.'

Around 2pm, I had sent a message to the dog sitter, asking: 'Any news? I've got in contact with your local pub you always said you went to quite a bit with Juno, they said I can put up posters around. Are you trying and helping to find her at all, and doing things like leaving food out and maybe her collar, as my partner says you took it off her?'

They replied: 'No need, but my eyes are always open for her. I'm up and down the trials every day, as well as other areas. Yes, I've left food out, and my t-shirt was on the line like I was told to do. No, I didn't take her collar off, I just had the tag off it.'

I frowned as I read this message. Why would they not think to put her name tag back on her collar?

'Ah OK,' I messaged back, 'me and my other dog went to the park again earlier, where I used to take her when living at the old house, and where I have seen that you have taken her too sometimes. I went all around the river area and railway line, and still nothing. She loves carrots, so maybe dropping some around the garden might get her to come back.'

They agreed and said they would get some, but I highly doubt they did – I don't think they would have bothered at all. In fact, I had a feeling they were lying about doing all the things being asked of them.

In the meantime, someone else had commented on one of the posts on a local group about Juno going missing. They had told me to message them as they had some more information. So I did.

At 5:15 that evening, my partner messaged me: 'I'm getting fed up with seeing the dog sitter posting everything about their dog walks, looking all happy as if nothing has happened.'

It was true – going by what we could see on social media, they were just carrying on with their own life, as if they hadn't been the one to lose her and if it was never their problem in the first place.

What kind of person does that, especially one who is meant to love dogs? How can someone who lost someone's dog act so calm and dismissive when they're supposed to care?

I also thought back to when I'd first got in contact with the dog sitter a few months previously, and I then looked back to some of the first messages we'd sent to each other.

When I'd asked if they could sit or board our young lurcher, they had stated: 'I'm sorry, we don't do sitting anymore as we don't have the space available. I can do walks at any time though, and maybe do a home sit at your house if that helps.'

I was in disbelief at the 'we don't do sitting anymore' comment – were they not just starting out then? I pondered on this for a while, and the only thing I could think of was that perhaps they'd done this before and something similar had happened... Well, maybe they were trying again – but, this time, using a different name.

None of it made any sense.

At this point – as I was extremely tired and stressed out – I ended up having a bit of an argument over text with my partner.

'You've been at work all this time while I've been stuck at home, stressing and over thinking things,' I messaged her. 'You've had your mind focused on other things and you've been talking to and interacting with actual people throughout the day. It's different for me.'

Ever since the pandemic started, I've hated being alone – a possibly by-product of PTSD from working on the frontline.

'You need a hobby, to have a project,' she suggested.

'I've been stripping the wallpaper,' I told her. 'If it wasn't for that, I don't know what I'd be doing, considering how mentally unstable I am now. I think I'll do a wider search tomorrow – it's a shame I must do it all on my own again.'

'I wish I could do more,' she replied, 'which is why I've been going hard online. Trying to talk to locals and gather interest.'

I then told her, 'I've been looking back at the photo the person took when they saw Juno by the railway – she was literally on the right-hand side of the bridge, on the tracks where the traffic lights are at the bottom of the road. She was so close to our house!'

'Oh, my days!' she exclaimed, 'that makes me feel even worse.'

At this point, I sent her a comparison screenshot from Google Street view. I also then said, 'The dog sitter said that Juno had her collar on.'

'That's so odd,' my partner replied, 'I swear they said she didn't have her collar on!'

'They have her name tag for some reason,' I messaged back.

So, it was now 11 that night, and the person who said they had more information about Juno replied:

'She ran past me on the bridge by the local pub. A minute later, a man came down – I was talking to another couple with a dog, so I was still there – and he asked if any of us had seen a big black lurcher dog. I said yes and that the dog was heading towards the train station. He went after the dog. Then an older woman came down and said that the dog had come out from nowhere, and they had hit the dog with their car by accident. She followed the man towards the train station too.'

When I read that message, my heart shot straight up into my throat as I sharply swallowed. The thought of Juno being hit by a car was almost too much to bear.

'I walked away,' they then continued in their message, 'but the car they were in pulled up by the entrance to the bridge. White car, I think. I didn't see anything else. I'm not sure if they had the dog or not. I hope this helps you find your dog.'

Incredibly upset and distraught, I replied: 'That was probably the dog sitter – she had escaped from the garden. So, did she run off after being hit? As another person had taken a photo of her down by the railway tracks.'

'I didn't see her get hit,' the witness explained, 'she was running when I saw her. The woman just told me that they had hit her with their car. So, she was running after being hit so it must not have been too bad. I wish I knew more. If there's anything I can do, please let me know. I'll ask the people I talk to down that way if they've seen anything. Hope she's OK.'

'Thank you for your piece of information,' I replied, my stomach still churning from hearing this dreadful news.

Half an hour later, I updated the admin from the missing dog's group on what I'd just been told. I then also sent a message to the dog sitter, sending them both a screenshot of the witness's message.

The dog sitters' reply was that they didn't know that Juno got hit by a car, only that she had headed towards the railway and that a man had seen her on one of the platforms. 'On arrival, there was no sign of her,' they ended.   Then that's when they again mentioned that they think she must have been taken in and kept by someone somewhere. 'Would have seen her by now surely – even if she's passed away somewhere, someone would've found her.'

As I read this message, I couldn't help but get even more angry.

Why were they so adamant about this theory of someone taking her in? Why would they keep saying this?

It made me start to feel unreal rage, in fact, that I replied, 'Well, I'm spreading the word, and if someone has got her and keeping her, I'll get the police involved!'

All the dog sitter replied with was: 'OK, my eyes are always open, and I've been busy the last few days, being out everywhere looking.'

I found that hard to believe.

'I might have another look tomorrow,' I told them, 'Around the spot where the person took the photo down by the railway.'

They said they would have a look there too, not realising how close where the photo had been taken and thought if she was there surely, she would've been seen by now.

'Just on the other side of the bridge, I Google Mapped it,' I told them, sending them the coordinates. 'I'll check out the area again tomorrow.'

They then agreed they would too.

'Thanks,' I politely said.

Then the dog sitter replied, 'No problem, it's the least I can do.'

Well, they weren't wrong about that.

'I hope she's found soon, I should be getting the posters tomorrow,' I then said. There was no reply from the dog sitter.

So, upon showing the admin of the missing dog's group what the dog sitter had said, they replied, 'I would get some posters up at the train station and around that area.'

'Yes, hopefully the posters will come tomorrow,' I agreed, before telling the admin that the dog walkers reply to the posters was 'no need.'

'Why would there be no need to put posters up?' I asked.

The admin replied, 'If someone did take her in, they can't hide her. The more people that know the area, the better. No proof now that she has been picked up.'

'True,' I messaged back, 'I'm going to be looking around the area more closely in the morning where the photo was taken by the railway. Hopefully she'll just be hiding somewhere nearby.'

'That's good, it looks like there are plenty of places there that she could hide out,' The admin stated.

So, I then decided to go to bed and prepare myself for the next day.

DAY 5 – FRIDAY 11ᵀᴴ MARCH 2022.

At around 9:20am on day five of Juno being missing, I messaged the admin from the missing dogs group: 'I've got to take my other dog to the vets today for a possible ear infection. Should I take a few posters there with me and ask the vets to put them up? Hopefully the posters will come by then, as his appointment is at 3:30pm.'

They replied, 'I think that would be a good idea, lots of people will travel to the vets so it will be good publicity for her.'

At quarter to 2 in the afternoon, I messaged back, saying: 'Actually, thinking about it, I don't think the dog sitter is telling us the whole truth about Juno running away from the garden. Maybe it was just an excuse to cover something up. But I won't think about it too much for now. We just need to get Juno found.'

The admin then asked, 'You don't know their full address, do you?'

I told the admin that I could ask the dog sitter, but that I didn't really want to talk to them at all as they irresponsibly lost my dog.

'It's just so I can have a look at the distance from their place to the train station on the map. Any posters yet?' the admin replied.

'Yes, I'll let you know if I find out,' I replied, 'and no, no posters yet. It's very frustrating as I could be out there looking for her, but instead I'm having to wait in as they had sent an email which stated that the posters could come anytime between 10am and 3pm.'

They replied, 'I hope they arrive soon.'

At 2:15pm, my partner messaged the group chat: 'The dog sitter is carrying on and still just posting about their other dogs they're out walking, as if nothing has happened. It's really beginning to irritate me.'

The admin replied: 'Yes, I can imagine. Any spare time they have should be spent on looking for Juno.'

I then told the chat, 'They say they are, but is still adamant that someone has found her and is keeping her!'

'If they suspect anyone, they should tell you. If not, then they need to keep looking,' the admin stated. My partner then added: 'I don't believe they're looking anymore; they look happy enough.'

I had soon messaged Juno's previous dog walker, 'Hi, how are you? I've still not seen any signs of Juno but looking at the photo of where she was last seen and comparing it to where we live now, as well as the potential dog sitters' house (the address, which was stated on their business page, anyway), I hope she isn't too far away. She can't be surely.'

Then came the reply, 'Hey, all good thanks. I haven't seen anything on my walk over your way either. I can only suggest going to where she was last seen. Take a blanket of hers or something, or an item of clothing. The scent may bring her back. Also take some food or treats – I'd look in the water too, just to be sure.'

'Thank you. I really hope she's okay. If she's gone forever, I'm going to delete the dog sitter out of my life completely and never speak to them again and may have to report them. If she's fine and we get her back, I know I'll never be using their services again, and worn others.'

'I really hope she's OK too. She's a lovely dog. So how did she escape? She's not usually nervous and she loves treats, so something must have happened. Have you had any information on how she got out?' they asked.

'They had told my partner at the beginning that they were letting Juno and their other dogs out in the garden, but someone had left the gate open; their dogs ran out the gate and came back, but Juno didn't come back. Upon telling me what had happened, they just said Juno had jumped over the fence in the garden. But checking where the dog sitter lives on their business page online, it looks as though it's just across the bridge on the other side. Someone has come forward who had witnessed Juno run past them heading towards the train station, which could be seen as a bit suspicious.'

'If they do live where the online business page states, then that means she wasn't at their house, which makes me even more suspicious,' I added.

'Bloody hell,' they replied, 'I just don't see why they wouldn't have been keeping a close eye on her to prevent it.'

'They just keep going on saying they think someone has found her and are keeping her. And I've told them I'll make sure everyone in this town knows she's my dog, so if she's seen with anyone else, it will be obvious they've stolen her.'

'Stupid question, but they don't have her, no?' they speculated.

That's what we had been considering – though we didn't want to think it possible. I just replied, 'No, not that I know of.'

It was now 4:15pm – after my dog's vet appointment – when I messaged the group chat, stating the posters still hadn't arrived. The admin replied, 'That's very unusual, they're normally very quick.'

'Hopefully, they will have arrived by the time my partner gets back from work later,' I told the chat before adding, 'I've just sent a message to the dog sitting stating how I feel and that I feel they are not fussed at all about Juno's disappearance. I also told them that '*she was lost under your watch!*'. Juno's previous dog walker suggested we go looking in the water around the area she was last seen, but I don't think I could face it if I was to find something I really don't want to see.'

I thought then for a moment, then sent another message: 'I've just had an idea, I still have one of her harnesses. Maybe if I get my other dog to sniff it, and then have another look around where she was last seen, my dog might be able to catch a whiff of her scent.'

The admin replied, 'No harm in trying.'

So that was my plan.

DAY 6 – SATURDAY 12TH MARCH 2022.

At half past 10 the next morning, Juno's previous dog walker replied to the message I'd sent the day before apologising that they thought they had since replied and said to maybe check if Juno had gone back to the dog sitter's house at all.

It was 12:20pm when I messaged back. 'The dog sitter is ignoring my messages, a bit suspicious again. The posters have arrived now, so I'll be going down to the pub (the dog sitters' local) and leave a poster up with them there.'

They suggested, 'I'd go back to their house and knock in person. Ask to see the location where she had 'escaped'. You have every right to, really, seeing as they've lost your dog.'

'True, I just need to know where they live; hopefully they'll know at the pub.'

'Oh,' they replied, 'so did they always pick Juno up and take her to theirs, rather than you drop her off there?'

'Yeah, they would always pick her up from mine.'

There was a distressing piece of news which came about, not about Juno, but about another dog which had been walked by someone in our area but the moment it got back to its owner, had sadly passed away. Of course, at this piece of news so close to home, my heart sank. Just what was going on? I hope Juno isn't dead too. I then tried not to burst out crying.

Could they be involved?

Surely there were all kinds of possibilities I'd like to think; maybe someone had been putting poison out and the dog had ingested it without any knowledge from the dog walker?

This was all so surreal what was happening. But as for the dog sitter, it was very strange, they hadn't been posting any updates on their online page for quite some time and weren't answering any of my calls or messages.

Just a bit odd.

This was, indeed, very odd, and it got me thinking about whether something like that had happened to Juno; some freak accident, perhaps, and the dog sitter was too scared to tell me. Making up other excuses.

I did show Juno's previous dog walker the last conversation I'd had with them, and they just replied, 'Wow.'

'Yeah, it's like they've not been making an effort at all,' I told them. 'And, if they had been chasing after her as soon as she escaped – like they had told me – then they would've found her where the witness took the photo of her last sighting. Railway lines go in a straight line anyway, so if by following it down, they'd have eventually tracked her down and found her, but I'm thinking they must have just given up and had other dogs' walks booked. Just kept saying, *'someone's probably got her and kept her; if she was dead someone would've found her by now.'*

Their reply was, simply, 'Very unprofessional.'

There was also speculation going around at the time about another dog walker who would drink when they were supposed to be looking after their clients' dogs, this same person would apparently go on about money and would pester the clients to pay them early.

Some people, I know after the lockdown and going back to work could be so desperate for someone to look after their dogs and everywhere else may be fully booked, they would have no other choice but to employ them. They would rather their dogs be out and about interacting with someone and possibly other dogs than be stuck in the house for maybe well over 10 hours at a time; that's not fair on any dog.

These are the people you need to watch out for. I had recently heard of another situation where the dog walker was apparently 'struggling' so begged the client to pay some before the dog walk, and then some after the dog walk.

Like whom the hell does that?

There are also a few out there who ask for cash so that it's invisible to the tax man.

What has this world come to?

One of my friends said they had a bad experience with a dog walker; they gave them a key to their place so they could come and let themselves in to collect the dog and they had left cash out for them on the side. As an experiment they put out more than when quoted for to see what the dog walker would say. The dog walker said nothing but 'thanks for the money.' But when they'd left out too little one time, the dog walker said, 'It was £30 for the three hours, not £20. I'd like the other £10 please.' It seems to be all about money these days and less about the care of the animals.

Sickening.

I had noticed a little bit of this happening with my dog sitter. At first, they seemed decent and got on well – I never try to judge anyone whatever their background may be – but when it involved money… that's when they started to get a bit cocky and change.

Juno's previous dog walker and I were still discussing the possibility of where the dog sitter lives.

'I keep wondering if that's actually where they live,' I agreed, 'though I do remember them saying they lived in a flat next to a garage, which I'm confused about also.'

'Hmm. How do you run a boarding place from such a small flat? You did know they aren't DBS checked and insured, right?'

'I did know that, yes. But they had informed me and reassured me that they were going to get things sorted once the business kicked off properly,' I replied.

An old neighbour knew them, and so did a few others and highly recommended them. So, we trusted it. We also like helping people out and we wanted to help them with their business growth and success. We were also, I will admit desperate – what with the hours we both work – and they were very flexible and accommodated to our needs at short notice too.' I explained.

Then they sent me a screenshot of a conversation between one of their clients and the dog sitter; they had asked if the dog sitter was DBS checked and if it was possible for the client to come to their place to meet, to discuss walking and sitting their dogs.

The reply was of the dog sitter stating they had only just started out and were not checked yet, then said, 'thank you for your interest though.'

'It seems to me,' I said, 'going by this reply, that they don't want people to come to meet them.'

This seemed very strange behaviour as I'm sure the dog sitter would jump at the chance to get a new client.

'Juno had a good bond with them apparently,' I added, 'which is also confusing – then why would she run away?'

I then sent a photo of Juno at the dog sitters' place, which they had sent me previously during one of the past dog sits.

Juno's previous dog walker commented, 'Looks to be quite high up from the window view.'

'That's why I'm thinking it might be a communal garden,' I said. 'Or did they even let her out in the garden? Did they actually lose her out on a walk? Or did they let a family member or acquaintance look after her whilst they were out taking other dogs walking? A mate that was probably drinking at the pub?' After all, on the day of Juno's disappearance, posting photos of the dog walks of that day, Juno wasn't anywhere to been seen in any of them.   'But we've made the local pub aware and handed in a poster for them to display,' I added.

I had sent the dog sitter a message the previous day, asking, 'Have you been looking today? It appears you're not really trying. You seem to be acting all like, *'Juno's gone missing, oh well, she's probably been found by someone and being kept by them,'* she was under YOUR watch!'

They hadn't replied until now, which was almost 24 hours later. They had said they've been looking for her every day and that they are *'gutted'* that she's gone missing.

'You can't assume I don't care,' I read on, 'I love dogs – all I've done is being worried about her – but at the same time, I've got to carry on with my life, if that makes sense?'

What was actually wrong with this human being?

Just seeing that they wrote they had to carry on with their life sent bolts of shock and anger pulsing through my body as shivers went down my spine and my blood started to boil through every single vein in my body – how dare they say that! That was pretty offensive to be quite honest.

I had to carry on with my life too! Working in a highly stressful environment and worrying every single hour of the day where the hell my dog was! Whilst they just got to relax and spend time chilling with family and take dogs out for walks, still earning money. I bet it would be a totally different story if I had been the one to lose one of their dogs!

'But I would've thought that you would at least post about her being missing or post her online missing poster on your business page,' I pointed out.

They just made the excuse that they had been sharing it on their personal online page. But to my astonishment when they sent a message that told me what had happened again, 'I never expected her to jump the fence… there was no way I could've stopped her or caught her. I went after her, but I went the wrong way as I didn't see which way she went, it all happened so quickly. I'd never intentionally hurt or lose anyone's dog. I loved her like my own.'

I felt extreme frustration upon reading these words. If that was the case, then why didn't they come straight over to ours the day she went missing, or even try to contact one of us? Why did we have to contact them to ask where she was?

They stated they had spent a lot of time together and how they *'bonded.'* Then came out with, 'It's hurting, actually, that you're now blaming me,'

What?!

'If I could have stopped her, I promise I would have, but I just didn't expect it,' they finished.

This sure felt like guilt tripping now, guilt tripping me about my own dog!? Making me feel small, and sorry for them, but it wasn't working. What with everything they'd said, and how they had reacted… it made me feel like they were trying to cover something up. I bit my tongue. I didn't want an argument and make an enemy.

So, with a deep breath in, instead, I just replied explaining how to re-post Juno's poster and said, 'I know you bonded with her, it's just so out of character for her to run away. Something must have happened. I just don't know what to do or where to look anymore!'

And that was the end of the conversation with them – at least for that day.

At 10 past 7, I told the admin from the missing dog's group that the dog sitter had finally replied.

I received this response: 'It's not good enough to say they didn't expect it, as a dog boarding house it must meet certain standards, such as fence height, that must be in place. Now the priority is to find Juno, and the dog sitter needs to help with that. They have an obligation since she was in their care.'

'That's what I had been saying to them, and now they're accusing me of blaming them – well, she was in their care, just like you said.'

'It's about taking responsibility,' the admin replied. 'I have worked with many dog owners whose dogs have been lost by dog walkers, and just about every one of them do all they possibly can to get the dog home.'

I then replied, 'I know, that's why I'm so shocked and surprised at the response and attitude from them: 'I have a life and need to carry on.' It's like me being at my place of work, reporting that a patient has just had a fall, but because my shift is ending, I say, *'It's not my problem anymore'* and leave. It's not what people do. It's mind-blowing to see how some people think and act.'

I messaged my partner to see if she could look for Juno on her way back from work: 'On your way home could you go looking around under the bridge? Juno's previous dog walker has suggested looking in and around the water too, but I don't want to be the one to find her if she's dead. If she is, I don't even want to think what I'll do! I keep seeing the dog sitter posting all their recent dog walks on their main page; I keep wanting to comment, 'Hope you don't lose them too!'

My partner replied, 'I'm getting angrier by the day.'

I still didn't know what was going on, but I knew one thing for sure: the dog sitter was definitely hiding something.

DAY 7 – SUNDAY 13ᵀᴴ MARCH 2022.

At around 5pm, Juno's previous dog walker sent me an alarming and stomach – turning post from a local online page.

It read: '**DOG REMAINS FOUND**.' And had stated that a local dog walker had found what looked like the remains of a dog on a walk up in the local woods. They had also said that another dog walker visually confirmed it, and then ended with, 'Hopefully this helps anyone who has lost a dog in and around the area.'

They had then posted the Google Maps coordinates of the area in which they had found the remains. After sending me this screenshot, Juno's previous dog walker added, 'May be worth looking into.'

So, I went onto the actual post online and read: 'Couldn't tell the breed, but to guess I'd say a greyhound or any other breed that would have short hair. I couldn't spot a collar, but then again, I didn't get close enough to check properly.'

I, of course, was frantic – absolutely riddled with fear, anger, and anxiety – especially when I had read the part about the remains looking to be a greyhound type. After all, Juno certainly fit that description, as a lurcher is part – greyhound.

I was also at work when I first saw this message, I had just started a nightshift, so I was trying my very best to remain cool, calm, and collected, composing myself and trying to not think too much about it for at least the time being. It was very hard to contain the amount of emotion I was feeling, but – having worked on the frontline through the toughest and most grueling parts of the pandemic – I had become accustomed to keeping everything in.

Later, when I had a few spare moments, I sent the post to my partner, after having also quickly looked up the area to see how far away it was from our house; it wasn't far at all and considering the amount of the Juno had been missing for, there was a possibility she could have easily made her way to the woods there.

My partners' reply was, 'It can't be Juno, right? I must believe it isn't.'

'I very much hope it's not,' I told her.

'What do we do? We must tell the admin in the group chat and go there tomorrow!' exclaimed my partner.

'If I wasn't at work right now, I'd go up there right now.' I had already messaged the person who had found the 'remains' and I had sent them a photo of Juno.

The message was: 'Hi, I saw your post about finding the dog remains. My dog sitter lost our dog on Monday 7th March, very close to where you said you had found the remains. Please tell me it wasn't her.'

They replied with, 'I'm very sorry to hear about this, we found the location of the remains here.' Then had sent me the exact coordinates. And continued, 'However, I was not able to tell the breed, unfortunately.'

Even though they had stated on their post it was a greyhound-type dog or a dog with short hair.

'Could you see any colour?' I frantically asked.

'No, sorry.'

'Ah OK, I really do hope that it's not her.'

My partner then said, 'It's too dark to go now. She'll be difficult to find. If that is her, I'm going to get so furious!'

'Are you able to get off work tomorrow?' I asked her.

'I don't know if I can; there are only two staff members on shift tomorrow. But I'll try. I literally feel nauseous.'

'Me too, this has got to be the worst week ever, when will this nightmare end?' I replied. 'I've been trying so hard to keep it all together at work. If it is her, I'll also blame myself for not looking hard enough – even though I had looked my absolute hardest – and in the right areas to begin with.'

Upon seeing the screenshot, I sent her, my partner replied, 'That's so far from us, it's insane!'

'It's not that far considering how long she's been missing now,' I pointed out. 'Almost a week – and she's a fast girl.'

I sent the group chat the dreaded post at around 6:30pm later that evening, and the admin replied, 'Hi, we are aware of this dog and are trying to get more information.'

I then told them that I'd messaged the person who had originally posted the information online and had sent them a photo of Juno.

They replied, 'OK, keep me updated and I'll do the same.'

'I will do, sadly, I'm at work tonight – if I wasn't, I'd be going straight up there to look.'

The admin said, 'I can only imagine.'

My partner replied to the group chat: 'I feel so sick, it can't end like this.'

'There will be a volunteer going up there midday tomorrow, she will be parking up near the pub. I will try and get a time from her in the morning. I will try and be there as well,' said the admin.

I then messaged the admin from the drones for missing dogs' group about the remains, telling them I had hoped it wasn't Juno.

They replied, 'Hi, yes, I hope so as well. Is there any way you can get up there to check?'

'I'm at work on a night shift tonight; if I wasn't I'd be going straight up there,' I told them. 'I'll be heading there after work tomorrow first thing in the morning though.'

'OK, keep me posted – and fingers crossed it's not Juno.'

My partner and I then had a long deep, dark conversation on my break about whether we should go on our own or have someone come with us.

My partner questioned, 'What do we do if it is her? Call the vets? The police? Who collects her body?'

'I'm not too sure, but I would take her to the vets and get her cremated – we could keep her ashes in a box,' I said, trying very hard not to focus too much on the actual words I was saying.

'I won't be able to do that,' my partner replied. 'I don't think I could actually carry her body like that – physically or mentally.'

I'd also messaged the dog sitter with this post about the remains that had been found, and they insisted on going up there with us in the morning. I told them they could, but then I thought about it for a while. After all, they hadn't even come over the day she went missing and hadn't been 100% honest about anything. So, I messaged them back and told them that my partner and I were going to go up there by ourselves. They then said that was OK and that they would find another way to get there.

That was hard to believe.

My partner said to me: 'Just tell them it's something we need to do by ourselves. It's not right for you to do this alone – I must come – I just can't look if it's her, it'll shatter my mind. I know you want to be sure, but this is going to be hard, and I'd like support.'

After that, I got back to work, for the rest of the shift, trying – and failing – not to think about the dog remains, lying out there in the dark and the fact that it may be Juno.

DAY 8 – MONDAY 14TH MARCH 2022.

It had now almost been over a week since Juno had gone missing, and it was the day we were going to look for the remains to find out if they belonged to her or not.

On the drive home from work, I was physically exhausted, - shaking with adrenaline and dread, trying to stay as calm as I could as I made my way home to pick up my partner.

While I drove, many different thoughts, questions and emotions were racing through my mind: What do I do if it's her? How did she die? Was she dumped there? Was she stolen? Who collects the body if it's her?

Just before 9am, I had received a message from the admin in the group chat, saying: 'Hi both, information from the person that found this dog is saying that it looks like it has been there for at least a week or more and is in very poor condition, just wanted to make sure you are aware of how unpleasant it may be. I will be going to help recover the dog at around midday, please let me know if you do go up there.'

I had said we were on our way up there right then and would let them know what we might find.

On our way to the dog remains, me and my partner were trying to stay as calm as possible – hoping for the best and thinking positively as possible – and we were glad to have our other dog with us, both for emotional support and in case he picked up any scents.

We parked up in a layby in the woods and then jumped out of the car, getting ready to walk and follow the coordinates on my phone, which were sent to me the previous night.

Slowly and carefully, we were thoroughly looking around and making our way through this surreal-looking woodland – which seemed to go on forever – and every time we spoke, the woods would carry our echo, it was so dense. It was also strange and so eerily silent.

When we had followed up to the point where the sat-nav on my phone had been leading us, we found a flattened, grassy span of land which opened invitingly.

There wasn't anything noticeable around this area that would lead us to believe there was anything dead here, within the soft earthy undergrowth – there simply wasn't anything there - or so we thought. But my dog started acting very strangely; he was refusing to walk up to a certain area, which made me think the remains must be somewhere close by.

Once we'd had a good and thorough look around, we hadn't managed to find any signs of the remains, my partner wanted to give up and turn back; she kept saying that it was because of our dog's reaction to that particular spot – there must have been something there at some point – but someone must have already come and picked the body up.

But being as stubborn and determined as I am, I wasn't giving up. However, I was adamant that we should stay here until at least we find something – whatever that something turned out to be.

So, we carried on walking a bit further downwards following the open woodland path, looking both left and right, scanning every single bit of ground and shrubbery we could cover.

Suddenly, from the corner of my eye, I spotted something on the right side of the undergrowth. I slowly turned towards it, shaking as I then sprinted over. It was a dead animal. I could make out. I then shouted over for my partner to come and see what I had found. Taking it all in, I could see that it was small to medium in size, it was a very pale tinted shade of grey in colour, and it had a wet but smooth look to it. It did have a similarity to some sort of canine.

I started to hyperventilate, but trying to compose myself at the same time, forcing myself to try and think slowly and clearly.

My partner shrieked.

For one thing, I was questioning if Juno was actually this size... had she shrunk due to the decomposing process?

I investigated as my partner stood her distance, and observed the carcass for a little while longer, pondering and scanning all around. As I was doing so, my whole body filled with nausea, dread and adrenaline. I could feel my throat closing and my heart beating up into my mouth as I gaged on the stench of death.

I was now fearing the worst. This carcass really did resemble a dog - a small whippet or terrier, maybe.

I walked my way slowly around it, investigating every single area of these remains. The head was very dog-like, and the teeth looked like the teeth of a canine. The body was curled up helplessly, and its smooth looking pale skin had seemingly been bleached by the beating sun. The legs were thin and bent inwards, but the paws looked like that of a cat, which I thought was quite odd as the rest of it didn't look at all like a cat. The tail was long and thin, just skin and bone. It looked kind of like a whippet's tail. As I stared closely at it, I racked my brain, considering and pondering what on earth this animal could possibly be.

I then started to search around a bit further afield, at which point I spotted copious amounts of what looked like clumps of ginger, fluffy fur scattered all around this corpse. Then I shouted in relief, 'This must be a fox!'

I couldn't begin to describe the amount of relief that then flooded through my body at this moment in time, making my heart pound so hard it was missing a few beats and my head started to pound. Juno must – and had to – still be alive! But where? I wish I knew.

Both extremely relieved, we then made our way back home, to continue with our search and spread the relief.

At around 10:20 that same morning, I received a message from the dog sitter – from their personal account: 'Any news?'

Then they said they had been trying to message me on their business account but said the messages weren't going through. I think somehow maybe they blocked me on their business page for some reason which led to me questioning again if they were hiding something.

'Yeah, we had no signal up in the woods. I don't think the remains are her, they looked like a fox.'

'Thank God for that,' they replied then asked me what time I was available later as they wanted to see me…

I told them anytime in the afternoon, then we agreed on a time.

Though a bit later I messaged back to ask if they could come over tomorrow instead. I didn't really feel like facing them after what had happened earlier that morning and the fact, I hadn't seen them at all since this incident had happened. Whenever they said they were wanting to come over, I got this weird feeling in the pit of my stomach.

A little while later, I sent the photos of the remains I had taken up in the woods to the person who had first posted about them and asked, 'Was this it? I think it's a fox.'

'Yes…,' came the reply. 'I think. Was it in the same spot as the coordinates?'

'It was a bit further along, down the path,' I explained.

I also showed them a screenshot of the map of the exact spot we'd found the carcass and compared how close it was to the coordinates.

They then replied, 'Yeah, that's probably it, would you confirm that it is definitely a fox? I might go and update my posts if that is the case.'

I replied, 'Yes, definitely. But I can understand from a distance it did look like a dog; a whippet or terrier type.'

I also then shortly after messaged the admin from the missing dogs group: 'It looks like it's a fox!! I am so relieved you wouldn't believe!'

'That is a relief! We will be checking though anyway.'

A few hours later messaged me back: 'Yes, a fox. I don't know if you got anywhere with the posters, but I would tend to put some up locally and around the area of your previous address.' They repeated.

'Yeah, we only went around the local town so far,' I stated. 'We have also managed to hand out a few posters to some local dog walkers. We'll also definitely be putting some around our old neighbourhood.'

'Great, at least there was some relief this morning.'

'Yes, so much! I just wish she would come home already.'

'Yes, we just need another sighting of her.'

'I just hope no one has stolen her, or that she's being abused by someone,' I worryingly stated.

'I don't think so, I don't think anyone would have caught her.'

'I do hope so.'

I then sent a screenshot of updated areas we'd been looking in, and – later that evening – I sent another message, asking, 'Any news on your end?'

'Nothing, though I was hopeful that with the weather getting warmer, we might get a sighting.'

'Yeah, me too. We had been talking to one of our neighbours earlier and they suggested we get in contact with the local kennels, which aren't at all far away from us. They said their dog was lost once, and was waiting by their front door, and another neighbour had seen someone come around the area in a van and picked him up.'

'They then took him to those kennels – I thought they were just boarding kennels.'

'I don't know of them… There's a specific dog rescue not too far and they have the council contract for stray dogs, and any found should go to them, worth a look though.' He informed.

'Yes, I'll be phoning them in the morning.'

As it was now getting quite late, I decided to set in for the night still exhausted and stressed.

DAY 9 – TUESDAY 15TH MARCH 2022.

This morning, I sent a message to the admin from the drones for lost dogs' group: 'I don't know where else to go looking. We've been all over these areas,' I then had sent them screenshots of the local areas which I had circled on the map.

They replied with, 'She's got to be local, is my thoughts. Have you got loads of posters out all over the place?'

'Yes, in local shops and all around – we even handed some to local dog walkers we've come across whilst out looking for Juno. Unless someone has stolen her, I don't understand why there haven't been any more sightings.'

'No, that is very odd,' they agreed. 'We would normally expect to have had at least one other reported sighting by now. Right, difficult question: do you trust the dog sitter?'

I replied, 'No, not 100%, not anymore. They just kept on about Juno had probably been found by someone and kept. Upon asking why they were saying that their reply was 'someone would've seen her by now or found her if she was dead.' I really don't know what to think anymore,' I admitted.

'It's all very strange why there have been no sightings since the day she went missing. She's not a small dog; she would stick out, being a big girl. This just doesn't make any sense.'

'I know,' I agreed, 'I just hope she's not being abused or being used for dog bait for dog fighting.'

This was one of my many fears concerning Juno, constantly circling my mind. I then told them that we had put up a poster at the dog sitters' local pub, also where they used to take Juno quite regularly. The dog sitter said she was very popular there, so hopefully, someone will know something.

'Hmm, that sounds very suspicious!' They snapped.

Does this sound suspicious? Everyone I speak to about it also says it all sounds very suspicious.

'Do I get the police involved in a possible dog theft?' I asked.

'It would be worth it for you to contact them and get an incident reference number,' they advised. 'You don't have 100% proof that she's been stolen, but it is a possibility, especially with no new sightings.'

'Yeah, I'll do that tomorrow to see what they can do,' I told them. 'I'll be once again going back to my old neighbourhood tomorrow too, to see where we can put posters up and to make sure if she has been seen around there or not.' I then mentioned that we did go around that area on the night Juno went missing but didn't manage to find anything.

'Posters are going to be the key here, so it's very important you poster, poster, poster. There are lots of people who are not on social media, so this is how we get reported sightings. Even put posters a few couple of miles, even as far as 15 miles – just get them out there!'

I had then told them that we had been out and about 5 miles each way putting some posters in shops but will be getting some poly pockets and tape tomorrow so that I can start putting posters up outside.

They replied, 'OK, that's a start, but also put them on lamp posts and telegraph poles. Call local taxi firms and ask their drivers to keep an eye open for her. Go to the local post offices' sorting office and put up a poster in there so all the post workers can keep a lookout too.'

'OK, will do. I'm also going to be requesting CCTV from the local council for the day she went missing – hopefully they can help.'

'Yes, good idea, and also anyone with a Ring Doorbell camera near to where she was staying.'

'Thank you,' I said, grateful for this helpful advice.

Later, at around 7 that evening, I messaged the group chat: 'No luck at the kennels. I don't know what to do anymore, or where to look. Do I put treats out everywhere I go?'

The admin had started by saying with the weather getting warmer they were hoping to get some sightings. Then said, 'I don't think leaving treats will help; all we can do at the moment is keep sharing on social media and putting posters around so we can get some possible sightings.'

'The other admin I'm in contact with, thinks that the dog sitter is suspicious,' I replied.

'Problem is, it is very difficult to approach them without any proof,' the admin pointed out. 'If we had CCTV coverage of anything, it would help.'

'I do need to find out about any CCTV in the area,' I agreed.

'Yes, anywhere she would've been walked… also, near the bridge and the railway station.'

'Do you think I'd be able to just Google the areas?' I asked.

'I don't think so, you need to drive – or better still, walk the area – and look for any cameras.'

'Ah OK. I know there were cameras in our old neighbourhood, but we didn't quite know if they were working cameras,' I told him.

'You can only ask.' They ended.

Hopefully the CCTV would give us some much-needed answers.

DAY 10 – WEDNESDAY 16TH MARCH 2022.

That afternoon, I messaged the group chat, letting the admin know that I'd looked up all the CCTV cameras in the local area.

'Looks like there are a lot around here, but as I expected none in our old neighbourhood – none that came up as working, anyway. We still need to keep going down that way. I've asked my partner to keep in touch with one of our old neighbours to check if Juno may have at some point turned up there.'

'My mind has just been all over the place,' I admitted. 'I can't think straight, and it's even starting to affect me at work – I'm starting to get so irritable… and just so generally fed up with life.'

'I can understand that. If you haven't already, it might be worth seeing if you can call the dog warden and tell her what's happened.'

We hadn't spoken to the dog warden as the dog sitter had told us they had reported Juno missing to them.

'I'll look it up. We also gave a poster out to someone we met walking, who worked for the council and said they'll put the poster up in the office at their workplace.'

'That's good. If you can get to talk with the dog warden and you can explain how Juno went missing, she may investigate it. When you call up you can tell her what happened.'

They then forwarded a screenshot of the council's dog warden's number.

'I will do, and hopefully I can get some CCTV footage of the day she went missing. The local council had sent me an email containing the details of the person to contact regarding the CCTV footage.' To which I sent a screenshot of.

'That's good, sometimes they don't allow the public to view any recordings, but they will hopefully check for you.'

'I did read that they might edit out the general public before letting anyone see any footage,' I told them, 'But maybe they can screenshot where they can see her on film and tell me what time it was captured – and where it looks like she was heading.'

A while later, I sent a message to the admin of the drones for missing dogs: 'I'm just waiting on the CCTV. I've been looking through a post on your page and saw about setting traps?'

'Yes, we need to know where she is before any traps can be considered,' the admin explained. 'The traps also have to be monitored 24 hours a day, and any wildlife that gets caught in it must be released immediately.'

'So, they can only be used if there has been a recent sighting?'

'Yes, but a trap is a last resort.'

'Ah, I see.'

'When we know where she is, food stations need to be placed in the area and we must be sure it is her eating from the stations. When this is confirmed, then a trap can be introduced.'

'OK,' I replied and proceeded to tell them that I had been going around where she was last seen every day calling her name, and that she loves carrots, so I've been leaving bits of carrots around the area, but it's hard to know for sure if it's her eating them. Then I asked, 'Have you got any advice? Until I get the CCTV footage, what can I do?' so desperate for answers.

'I've done the clothing item in the back garden, I've been going around with posters, I've informed the railways… would you say it's suspicious that the dog sitter said they have Juno's name tag?'

'Why would they have her name tag!?'

'I know, right!? Why not put it back on her collar if it had fallen off? It's especially annoying as it had my address and phone number on it, in case she got lost.'

What a coincidence.

'That's very odd.'

'I'd noticed it was missing a while back,' I continued, 'but I just thought it must have fallen off on a walk or when she was out playing with other dogs. As I remember as a child, our Labradors were always losing them.'

That evening, I asked my partner to try calling the local railways, again. She said she would call them tomorrow, and I insisted her to call them now! In the end, with some persuasion she had managed to get hold of them and told me: 'They will make a refence number for us and they will send some people out to look for her if she's spotted.'

This is what they said to me when I had informed them the first time.

'So, no one has seen her? Or will they check with their colleagues?'

'They will investigate and ask around,' she said.

'I do hope the council has some CCTV footage of Juno.' I then sent her a screenshot showing the number of CCTV cameras around our area.

'I didn't realise there were so many,' my partner replied.

'I hope the council can send me CCTV tomorrow – or at least tell me they've found something.'

I was on a night shift at work again, but it was getting harder and harder – what with the long hour plus drives to and from work, the stress of the job, and having worked on the frontline throughout the pandemic. And now – with all this happening with Juno – I just didn't know how much more of this I could take.

Little did I know of what was to unfold upon this night shift…

DAY 11 – THURSDAY 17TH MARCH 2022.

It was at exactly 3:57am in the morning, I had received a private message from someone I didn't know.

It read: 'Hi, I'm one of the railway workers. On our shift last night, I believe we found your dog whilst working.'

Just reading these words, I was in disbelief, so I double checked. I lost my breath and it felt like my heart had stopped beating for what seemed like a whole minute.

I carried on reading the message with tears welling up. 'The dog was in a bad way, full of cuts and open wounds. We fed her and gave her water, then safely got her off the railway where she was, and she was then taken to an emergency vet not far away. I have no further information now, but I'll message you as soon as I can find out the name of the vet and any other updates.'

I started to go into complete shock. Then started to hyperventilate.

As I was reading this, my heart sank deep into the pit of my stomach; I almost stopped breathing, felt extremely faint and my heart was pounding at what felt like 100 miles per hour. I knew then immediately as this news hit me, that it must be Juno! Having been found on the railway!

'Really?! Please could you give me the details for the vets when you can? Thank you!' I was frantic and shaking as I messaged back.

'Of course, I will, sorry to message so early, I've just got back from my shift,' they replied.

But I was so glad that I had been on a night shift to have received the message when I did. 'I've texted the relevant people requesting the information, but it may be later in the afternoon before I hear anything. I'll get back to you asap!'

'That's fine, I'm on a night shift at the moment,' I explained. 'Thank you, again!'

'No problem at all honestly,' they replied.

'I've been so stressed out and have been worrying so much about her. Please could you pass my number onto the vets when you know which one, she's at?'

I then sent over my number.

They then replied, 'She's a lovely little dog, so sweet. She was fed and given water immediately and then straight to the vets. No problem. As soon as I can, I'll get the vet's name and connect you both.'

I was still in utter shock, tearful to the point of crying as I replied, 'Yes, she is a lovely sweet, gentle dog. I've missed her so much!' I was welling up and shaking as I messaged back.

'I can imagine! I've now texted all the people I can, just waiting for their replies. They may be sleeping now, but in the afternoon is the latest we will sort it out.'

'Thank you!'

I continued back to work trying to keep my mind focused for what felt like an hour but was 10 minutes and, a bit later, they had sent me the name of the vets Juno was at along with their contact details!

'Thank you! I'll ring them first thing in the morning when I get home from work.'

The railway worker then asked if I could send them any updates, just for their own piece of mind.

'Yes, I will do.' Still in a state of shock, not believing what I had just read but going along with it anyway.

I then sent them a photo of me and Juno cuddling on the sofa together. 'I've missed my cuddles with her so much; she'd lie on her back leaning into me, she would also flick her paw if she wanted me to carry on stroking her.'

'She's beautiful, I'm hoping she can make a full recovery. Such a gentle dog, so lovely.'

'Me too, and she is. I really do hope that the cuts and other injuries aren't from something bad like abuse – or being forced into dog fighting,' – which was always the worst situation always playing on my mind, - 'and then being left for dead. Was she found close by from the vets?'

They had then replied saying that Juno had been found exactly where the person who took the photo of her when she was spotted on the railway, and the vets were the only emergency vet that could see her. Then saying about her injuries, 'In my opinion, she probably got into a fight with a badger or a fox. But you'll find out more in the morning.'

I couldn't believe it.

'We've been walking around that area every single day looking for her! We never heard or saw anything!'

'She was curled up in some bushes, so you wouldn't see her unless you were on the actual tracks.'

By now I had started physically shaking. 'Ah I see... I don't want to think about or want to know how long she's been there, just curled up like that. Is she really thin?' – They had then sent me a couple of photos of where and when they had first found Juno. The look on her face as she looked up at the workers who rescued her broke my heart and in the very first photo, it looked as if she had just given up on life and was just ready to die.

'She was super thin, but we fed her two tins of dog food and some chicken and gave her water.'

'Thank you so much!'

'Honestly no need for thanks, - broke my heart seeing her like that. We stopped all work immediately and got everyone informed and we did the best we could. Please let me know how she is when you hear from the vets.' Then told me they were off to get some sleep and Juno was in their thoughts.

'Thank you so much, again!' I messaged back. 'If you weren't there at the time you found her, she may not have made it much longer and would've just died there. You and your colleagues saved her life! I will let you know. I'm going to get back from work, get my partner, and get over there as quickly as we can. I don't care how much money they want to get her better, I just want her to be OK.'

I later found that the railway worker had put a post up on social media about Juno, trying to track down the people she belonged to: 'Hi guys,' the post read, 'this little one was found last night by rail workers on the railway tracks in some bushes. The dog has been taken to the vet. If anyone is living in and around where we've found her and could share, I'd be very grateful to help it be reunited with its owners.'

After talking to the person who assisted in helping find 'Juno', I sent the group chat a screenshot of what I'd just been sent by the railway worker.

At 5:50am, the admin soon replied, 'Phone this number now.' And then sent me a screenshot of the vet's details. 'It will be these vets; they are a 24-hour veterinary hospital.'

I immediately went off to find any empty room I could on the ward to call the vets; shaking in anticipation and fear of what news I was about to hear. Then, with my trembling hands, I eagerly phoned their number.

I was on hold for quite some time, each minute felt like 10 as I was awaiting a response. The 'phone on hold' music was making it even worse, and I was starting to associate my anxiety with this piece of music.

Eventually, to my relief and to break this anxiety, someone answered the phone. I described to them what Juno looked like and sent some photos over email to make sure it was her. Both to my relief and concern, they confirmed it was her; that it matched her description exactly! They told me she'd been so gentle, letting them examine her and do what they had to, even though she was clearly in a lot of pain. She was such a trusting dog, they said.

I suddenly started blubbering to the woman on the other side of the phone as they told me the extent to her injuries; my voice was quivering and breaking up. They said she had many soft tissue injuries and a very severely damaged back leg. I told them, my voice quivering, 'Yes, there had been a report of her being hit by a car.'

That was the most emotional phone call I have ever had to endure in my life. I felt emotionally, mentally and physically exhausted – and my shift wasn't even over yet.

I soon messaged the group chat at 6:30am, stating ecstatically, 'Yes, it is her!'

'How is she please?' the admin concernedly asked.

'Not in a good way,' I replied. 'She's got major soft tissue damage and a load of cuts all over her body. She'll be needing extensive surgery on one of her back legs. I will be calling them up again when I get back from work later, around 9am. Then I'll pick up my partner and hopefully we'll be able to go straight there to see her.'

'Poor girl,' the admin said, 'praying she will be OK.'

'I do hope so *fingers crossed* I just can't believe the number of times I must have walked right past her without knowing. She's probably been curled up like that since the evening of the 7th of March!' I then sent the admin the photos the railway worker had sent me.

'Not easy to spot sometimes. Please let me know how she is when you have further news.'

'I will do.'

They then thanked me.

'I just don't know what to do about the dog sitter now,' I claimed, 'is there any legal action I can take? What can I do? They didn't even bother to go out looking for her!'

The admin suggested for me to just report it all to the local council and the dog warden. 'As a boarder, they must be licensed by the council and should have their premises inspected. Just see what the council and dog warden say. They also must have insurance for this sort of thing.'

'I think they've closed their business account down online.' I told them.

'Or it's been closed down by the council,' they pointed out.

'Yeah, possibly. Or maybe they've blocked me again.'

'The council need to know.'

'Yes,' I agreed. 'I'm just now going to have to work out how to afford their stupid mistake first!'

I was eventually back home at around 9:15am that morning and I phoned the vets straight away. One of the reception staff spoke to me. They said that they will need payment for her treatment so far and there are three options that the vet would speak to me about later. I really didn't want to hear the options if it meant anything bad and what if we couldn't afford the treatment? We would have to choose that worst possible option, and the thought of that I then just burst out crying. Why must this be so hard? I haven't even slept properly for over a week, and I was just now at breaking point. I didn't need this at all.

I had checked my phone at around 9:30am, the dog sitter had tried to call me as they'd seen the posts all over the online platforms about Juno being found.

I wasn't feeling in the mood to talk to them, let alone even think about them.

Juno was my priority now.

After acknowledging the missed call, they then messaged me the screenshot of the online post, but all they sent after was a 'thumbs-up' emoji... like, what the hell?! Patronising or what? And they could clearly see from the photos how bad of a condition she was in – very strange.

At around 9:45am, once I managed to calm myself down a bit, I had received a reply from the rail worker saying that they were just so glad they got her to the vets in time and asked if I had an update.

'I'm just so grateful, you wouldn't believe!' I messaged back.

'They said they'll call me back with a time to go and see her, I'm going to take her blanket and a soft toy so she can feel a bit more comfortable and with familiar items.'

'That would be lovely, she'll be so grateful for that. Fingers crossed for a speedy recovery.'

They then sent me a few more of the photos they'd taken when they'd found her. They were absolutely heart breaking; I was quivering as I showed them to my partner as she burst out crying.

The photos showed the exact area where she was found, and how she was found; curled up lifeless in the bushes – looking like she had already accepted her fate – ready to die.

I soon sent these photos to the admin of the missing dogs group.

'I hope she'll be OK,' the admin sent back.

'I hope so too,' I replied. 'I can't even bring myself to look at the first photo if at all for long at all; it looks like she had accepted her fate and was just waiting there to die.' But in the photos where she'd acknowledged the railway workers, she looked as if she was very pleased and grateful that somebody had come to rescue her.

'It's totally heart breaking,' the admin agreed, 'but she's a fighter;

I know she'll have a speedy recovery.'

'I just keep blaming myself for not looking hard enough,' I messaged, unable to shake off that feeling of guilt.

'You weren't to know,' the admin replied, 'none of us could have known exactly where she was. Just concentrate on getting her well again.'

'Definitely, I will for sure.'

'Are you at the vets now?' they asked.

'No, not yet.' I replied. 'I've called them. They said they'll call back with a time I can go and see her, as the nursing team are having handover now, so I just spoke to one of the vets.'

'OK, let me know when you have any news.'

'I will do, don't worry.'

I had also sent Juno's old dog walker the screenshot of the message from one of the rail workers who had found Juno, their reply was: 'Amazing stuff. Glad she has now been found.'

'Yes, she's safe at the vets now, getting the best treatment. I'll be going to see her later; I was literally crying on the phone earlier when I called the vets up when I first heard where she was.' I then carried on telling them that the vets had told me that Juno had been such a good dog, letting them do anything and everything they had to do to her, and so gentle too.

'That's good. She's probably very scared, bless her.'

'Yeah, she has extensive injuries though, and I feel so bad. She had probably stayed there, in that exact same spot she was found, curled up in the bushes, for over a week! I've walked past that area loads of times, and I couldn't see or hear anything. I should have jumped the fence and gone onto the railway tracks myself.'

It was then at that moment, at around half past 10, I received a phone call from the vet, they told me more about the extent of her injuries and how serious they were; it was either for her to have surgery to fix the fractured ankle on her back leg, amputate it or – put her to sleep. I could NOT put her to sleep! I had to save her! They then also told me that I could come and see Juno later in the afternoon, any time after midday.

Now even more upset, I really didn't know how much more of this I could take.

I immediately sent Juno's previous dog walker a message: 'It's not looking good at all.'

'No? In what sense?' they questioned.

'Her ankle is so badly fractured, they'll either need to do extensive surgery to repair it with metal work, which could cost anything over £8k, or amputate her leg which would still cost a lot... or, the worst option, and morbidly the cheapest, which I know and can tell you is definitely out of the question: put her to sleep.'

'Oh no. I'm so sorry,' they sent back.

'This is all the dog sitters' fault.' I told them.

'Have they contacted you since she was found? Do you have insurance for her?'

'Yeah, they tried this morning but I'm not I the mood. I don't particularly want to speak to them right now. And no, I don't have insurance, I never expected anything like this to happen to such a young and healthy dog. I do regret it, but I do have insurance for my other dog as his breed is known for having health issues. I'm just going to have to see what loans I could possibly take out as the vets don't seem to do payment plans, which I think is not moral at all. They only seem to care about the money, not the circumstances.' I know it's the big companies who only think about the money – the vets and other staff are only just doing their job.

'Bless you. The dog sitter should be paying for it! I'm sorry but she was under their care and responsibility. Their insurance should cover it.' And then they asked if I was going to go for the amputation and asked what the cost of that was. They also suggested a local animal charity.

'I know, they should! Yeah, I think amputation will be the best option. For everything, the vet said that it should cost around £6 - £8k.'

'Bless her. Poor thing. I would be in touch with the dog sitter regarding the cost, to be honest.'

'Yeah, I definitely will be.'

'Message the owner of the charity I told you about,' they suggested.   'Explain to them what happened. They are good and will do loads to help.'

'Thank you. Do they have an online page?' I asked.

'The vets can contact them if needs be, and they should have one, yeah.'

'Cool, OK.'

And with that, Juno's previous dog walker sent me a screenshot of the contact details and sent a message.

'She would have to be in their care though for some time, so be prepared, OK?'

'That's OK,' I replied, 'as long as we could still visit.' I don't know how I could cope not seeing her for an extended amount of time and seeing her recovery.

'Not entirely sure how it works in all honesty. But they do loads of fundraising and that, so they'll be great. Give Juno a hug from us please, when you see her.'

'Thank you – I've sent a message now, and I will do.'

Next, I messaged the admin from the drones for lost dogs' group about the news: 'I've found where she is!! I'm so relieved! The railway workers who found her, one of them sent me these photos.' I then sent them the photos of when she had just been found.

'Oh my god, that's amazing news! I'm so happy for you and her!' they replied.

'I know. I feel physically sick, but relieved,' I told them. 'I'm probably going to burst out crying when I see her later on.'

'Aww bless, don't worry – I would be the same. Did they say how bad she was? Had she been hit by a train?'

'At first, they said that it was a dislocation and soft tissue injuries. Now they're saying she may need surgery. I just keep blaming myself for not going down onto the railway tracks myself; I could've found her after a couple of days or less.'

'Don't blame yourself, these things happen,' the admin tried to reassure me.

'The main thing is she has been found and she is receiving treatment for her injuries. She'll be back home with you before you know it. I've now updated the post on our group page for you.'

And I thanked them for doing so.

I had then reported the news from the vets to the rail worker who had found her and messaged me earlier that morning: 'I have just spoken to the vets on the phone, and it's not looking good. Her ankle is severely fractured in many places and is so bad that she'll either need surgery – which will cost around £8,000 + - or an amputation. The other, last option and the one we will not be doing is to put her down.' I messaged with a tear in my eye.

'That's awful news,' the rail worker replied, 'could amputation be a viable option?'

'Yes,' I said, 'that's the option we'll be discussing – and probably choosing.'

'Yeah, it's amazing what the vets can do these days,' reassuringly replying.

After a long and busy morning – and still no sleep – we were on our way now to the vets. The drive wasn't pleasant.

When we had arrived at the vets, finally at 12pm – after going to the wrong place – they prepared us for how bad a condition Juno was in, and – as I sat in the reception room waiting with my partner – I was breathing slowly, deeply, in and out, physically shaking and internally panicking.

It seemed like we had been waiting for about an hour when eventually, they called us up and took us through into the ICU kennels, where the smell of disinfectant and other chemicals burnt my nose. Then we arrived at her kennel, where Juno lay lifeless, - she was staying in and receiving treatment.   It was the most sorrowful sight I had ever witnessed. She was just lying there, limp and seemingly utterly lifeless. Her deep brown eyes slowly shot towards my direction as our eyes locked into each other's, as I came into view of her. I could see every single bony prominent in and all over her body; she was so, so thin and totally emaciated. This was something I had only ever witnessed on TV – never in real life.

I had to pinch myself to make sure I wasn't dreaming - as I had become a bit delirious from lack of sleep. She had a very distressing open wound on her right back leg – this was the fractured ankle, which was extremely distended and swollen. She also appeared to have many scrapes and injuries on her other leg and all over her head there were bite wounds. She was hooked up to a long cabled, clear drip which was coming from one of her front paws; this was pumping in vital medication keeping her alive.

Having never seen anything like this before right in front of my very eyes, it was a colossal amount of trauma to the system.

Trying to pull myself together and back into reality, I perched down slowly next to her, and she gave me another deep, longing gaze into my eyes – with her own sunken brown dull eyes – as I grasped her paw gently in my hand. I couldn't really caress her body as she was all literally just skin and bone. She was also so frail and weak; she could not stand up at all.

She soon appeared to then recognise me, then let out a weak whistle of a whine, and then that was the very moment I couldn't hold myself together any longer – I started to cry – I was crying with sadness for poor Juno, and with pure disappointment at the dog sitter. I caught at the corner of my eye that the vet even had to turn and walk away, as he too was welling up; I could also hear it in his voice as it started to break as he spoke to us.

We spent a good long hour or so with her. I scratched and rubbed her side gently, and she then did the little paw flick that she would usually do when she wanted us to keep stroking her and giving her attention. We knew from that moment she was going to be a fighter; she just gave me that determined gaze.

The veterinary nurses suggested we set up a GoFundMe page and said these are normally very successful. I'd never have thought to create a GoFundMe page as I feel bad. But I know this is for a good cause – to save Juno.

My partner told us all that the director of the local railways was interested in doing a story about her being found on the railway tracks, as it could be quite popular, and he felt like he had to do something for the dog that was found near the railway.

Before we left Juno to get some much-needed rest, I wrapped her up in her blanket from home and brought in her soft toy. I kissed her on her head and told her we would be back to see her soon. She whined softly on our departure.

On the drive back home, my partner was trying to set up the

GoFundMe page for Juno on her phone. It wasn't until a while later when we were back at home, she then successfully created it. There were problems with verification and linking up to the accounts.

As soon as we got the page set up, we then set out and started spreading the word.

I tried to tweet this story to a few well-known celebrities, as I knew they love dogs, hoping that they would help.

My partner then suggested sending her the photos of the rescue on the railway, as she said the director for the railways wanted to use them for his story.

At around this time, I sent a photo of Juno – cuddled into her blanket with her soft toy at the vets – to the rail worker who had messaged me.

'Sorry for the late reply,' they sent a while later. 'Oh my god, she looks 1,000 times better – love her! She's such a pleasant dog. When I get into work tonight, I'll show the boys that picture, everyone has been asking about her! The most famous and loved dog on the railways, that's for sure!'

'That's OK. Yeah, she's so sweet,' I agreed. 'Aww yeah, she is! We've now got a GoFundMe page going – please could you share it around if you haven't done so? Vets are very unfair; they want part of the money right then and there... no choice of payment plans.'

'Wow, that's disgusting of them, surely they should have morals?!'

'I know, even at the Super vets' surgery, they offer payment plans – I'm hoping to get my dogs BOAS (Brachycephalic Obstructive Airway Syndrome) surgery done there.'

They then said how disgusted they were at that fact, then asked how much the amputation option would be.

'I know, I don't know why all veterinary practices can't all offer payment plans like Noel Fitzpatrick's'. It's because he truly cares for the animals, way before the money. He would try his hardest to save Juno's leg, I bet. And I can't remember exactly, but the vet said the amputation and the whole treatment would come to around £6,000 - £8,000, give or take depending on after care and complications.'

'That's awful,' they replied. 'I've just noticed the GoFundMe page you set up – I'll send it to my boss, and I'll show the boys. We'll all donate something when we finish work.'

'Thank you so much!'

'No problem at all.'

And at this point, I'd messaged one of my work colleagues whom I was going to be working with: 'I'm sorry if I'm no good at work tonight, I've been so stressed, and have had no sleep. I did call up work earlier to say I'm probably not physically and mentally fit to come in for the night shift tonight, but apparently, I must come in as there is only one other healthcare assistant in, and they are now doubling up patients' rooms!? I don't know how I'm going to get through it.'

They replied, 'Oh mate, that's horrible. I was thinking about that to be fair. We are going to be fine. You are an excellent healthcare assistant, and I will help as much as I can! I really hope they'll get us more healthcare assistants though.'

'Thank you, I know you are amazing like that,' I replied, grateful. 'I just hope I don't snap; I've not even had any time to properly process the two years of working through the pandemic. I really hope so too.'

'Yeah, I get what you mean, it's just been an ongoing battle, I find,' they messaged back, 'but we always do our best and we always help each other. Teamwork makes the shift go smoothly. (I cannot say 'makes the dream work' lol). Let me know if I can do anything else for you.'

'Thank you.' I was most grateful.

'Juno is being looked after, try not to worry too much about her. You need to be strong for her,' she told me.

'Yes, she is. I'm going to see if I can visit her again in the morning on my way home from work.'

'Yeah, that should be fine, shouldn't it? You're amazing and very strong!'

'Thank you so much, see you later.'

I felt very supported.

The admin for drones for missing dogs had very thoughtfully and kindly put up a post about Juno being found and about the GoFundMe page, which stated: 'Group, this is something we don't normally allow, but I feel this is something we can and need to help with. I have been in constant contact with Juno's owner, and know he is a hard-working lad in the healthcare profession. As we all know, the pay isn't that good. Juno's owners have searched high and low in the days since Juno has been missing. Thankfully, she was found in the early hours of this morning by railway maintenance workers and then taken to the emergency vets.

Juno has a lot of injuries and is going to need to have her leg amputated at a staggering cost of over £7,000! They have started a fundraiser to help towards the vet's fees for this treatment. If you can spare a couple of pounds to go towards this treatment, Juno and her owners would be very grateful. Please donate on the following link and let's get this beautiful girl the treatment she needs.'

I felt so overwhelmed reading this, they really cared so much about Juno and helping us!

There were 312 reactions to this post and 291 comments.

I thanked them ever so much for doing this, as I didn't ask them to, and they didn't need to.

Now we just needed to raise the rest and get Juno the treatment she so desperately needed and deserved.

We shared the GoFundMe page hard and fast in multiple groups all over social media, and anywhere else we could – there was no way we were going to give up on Juno – and it wasn't long before we'd raised £1,000!

'We now have £1,200!' My partner texted me, as I, again was back on another night shift, 'and now £1,400! We're even getting American's donating!'

So, my partner kept me updated throughout my shift.

Then, at 11:40pm that night, I checked the GoFundMe page to find, to my amazement and shock, the donations had gone up to nearly £5,000!

We were already almost there within 24 hours!

I was definitely positive Juno was going to have her surgery!

<u>DAY 12 – FRIDAY 18TH MARCH 2022.</u>

I phoned the vets again this morning for an update on Juno. I then received a message from the admin for drones for missing dogs at around 10am: 'Hi, how is Juno this morning? I'm so happy to see our members have come up trumps yet again, I'm sure this has taken a lot of the financial burden away from you. The important thing is to get Juno the treatment she needs and deserves and hopefully she'll make a full recovery. I hope you didn't mind me telling them you were a healthcare worker. What would be good is if you can keep the post updated with photos of Juno; I'm sure everybody would like to see how she's getting on.'

'Thank you ever so much for doing that,' I replied thankfully, 'it had made such a difference. I will keep the post updated. I called the vets this morning after work and they said she's comfortable, and that she's been eating and drinking well. I'm off to see her again at 3:30pm today!'

'Aww bless her, that is so good to hear,' they said. 'OK yes, keep the post updated – the money's still coming in, so they'll want updates and pictures, if possible, that would be good. When are they planning on doing the operation?'

'Definitely, I will. And when she's got enough strength and has put on a bit of weight. It's extremely upsetting how thin she really is,' I told them. 'They've had to start slowly refeeding her, little and often.'

'I will have to come and meet her one day when she is home and better. I don't live too far from you', they stated.

'Yes, definitely.' I agreed.

I then went to visit Juno at 3:30pm. The vets lead me straight through the back to the ICU room, where Juno was resting. As soon as she saw me her eyes lit up with joy. And then I sat with her for some time stroking her and holding her paw. I didn't want to leave her again, but I had to.

Later that day, at around 6pm, I sent some photos of Juno that I'd taken when I'd visited her later that day. The images showed the left side of her thin and sunken head and sad-looking eyes, there were puncture wounds from a possible animal attack, and she was wearing a special little vet coat as she was so thin.

'Aww bless her, I wonder what happened, poor baby,' the admin replied.
'They had to shave her head to clean the nasty wounds,' I explained.
'How is her leg? I can see there's a lot of damage on the one leg, and the other leg has nasty gashes on it, poor thing.'
'I'm trying to figure out if her hind legs look bad in the photo that the person took of her at the railway tracks. I'm going to try and get to the bottom of what happened to her face; I'm going to ask the dog sitter if there may have been a possibility that a dog may have attacked her to make her run away like she did. She was obviously scared.'
'Hmm yes, that is a possibility,' they agreed. 'It's very strange, and they do look like bite marks. Her ear looks like it has been bitten as well. What dog do they have?'

I then soon sent over a photo the dog sitter had taken one time when looking after Juno at theirs, which featured both their dogs.
'What is it?' they asked. 'A staff-cross?'

'I think so, yeah.'

'I've just looked at the wounds on her hind legs again and they do like bite wounds – bloody hell, that poor girl. If a train had hit her, there would be broken, crushed bones, but I don't think there are any, are there?'

'Her ankle is badly fractured, possibly by the car – a witness had reported Juno getting hit by a car,' I explained.

A while later, I sent the photos to the admin from the missing dog's group too.

'Poor girl, she will come back from this though,' they replied.

'Definitely. She's a fighter!'

'Would like to meet her when she has recovered if possible.'

'Yes, definitely.'

Now Juno simply had to get better – she had so many fans wanting to meet her!

DAY 13 – SATURDAY 19TH MARCH 2022.

The next day I did my new usual routine of calling up the vets and checking on Juno, and of course going and seeing her. They said she was comfortable still and I could see her at 4pm.

All I did in between this time and waiting to visit her was get worried and getting so anxious – as she's not out of the woods yet.

4pm couldn't have come round any quicker, and it was time to visit her again.

On arrival at the vets, I sat down in the reception area until I was called.

The veterinary nurse finally called me up and I followed her into a small room at the end of the corridor. It read 'family room' on the door.

As I walked into the room, I could tell that this was the room specifically where people go when the vets put their pets down. My stomach dropped. What were the vets going to tell me? Was she not doing very well? Were they going to tell me that she must be put down?

I slowly placed myself on one of the sofas they had in that room and anxiously waited and looked around the room, imagining what my response would be, hearing the worst news possible. Upon looking around, I spotted another sign of what this room was made for – I saw a jar of chocolate which had labelled on it 'All dogs deserve to taste chocolate before they go to heaven.'

I started welling up.

Trying to distract myself, I soon heard some limping paws walking along the outside corridor!

It was Juno!

As the door opened, I immediately stood up. There she was, so weak, so thin and had a general sadness about her. The vet nurse placed a fleece blanket on the floor for Juno to lie down on. Then left us alone.

I kneeled slowly and stoked her face as she looked at me with deep longing eyes. It still upset me how thin she was and how weak. She had a little yellow bandage with a green paw print design wrapped around her bony fractured ankle. She was wearing her little navy coat to keep her warm and hide how horrendously thin she was. Her little white tip on her nose had gone. It was now bright pink and sore. She had her teddy with her and was clutching it up to her neck. Her tail looked as if it had been bitten off or ripped off – the bone was sticking out from the tip. It was a while when Juno felt a bit happier and tried to roll onto her back for me to scratch her belly, but because she was so weak, she only managed to turn slightly. She then got ready to stand up, with an almost silent moan she slowly stood at her feet. I decided to let her have a walk around as I sat back on the sofa. Juno then tried to get up with me on the sofa; it broke my heart that she was trying so hard but couldn't get up. I kept reassuring her she would get better, and everything would be OK.

At 6pm that evening, the admin from drones for lost dogs messaged me: 'You need to change the fundraiser to £7,000. Not sure, but I've been told that if the donations go over the set amount, GoFundMe keep them?'

'Ah OK, I'll change it,' I replied.

'I'm not sure mind – I've never heard of this, but somebody just messaged me to tell you to up it for that reason.'

'Yeah, I haven't heard that either. I'm not sure how to change the fund amount but I'll have a look, thank you. I hope it's not true.'

'Yeah, me too. Wow, I've just been looking at their fees…

shocking!'

'Yes, I know, GoFundMe seem to profit from tragedies, which I think is a bit wrong!'

A little later that evening, I messaged the admin in the group chat and sent some more photos I had taken during my visit. The first photo was of Juno lying on her left side lying with her little teddy; her face was recessed, and she just looked very hopeless and sorry for herself. The next photo was of Juno trying to get up on the sofa with me, and the last one I had sent of her face looking so upset and depressed.

The admin asked, 'How is she today?'

'A bit better, still quite weak but she needs to put on a bit of weight before surgery. She has no issues with eating and drinking, so that's a bonus.'

'Yes, she needs to put a little on so that she will be stronger. It's a good sign that she's eating and drinking.'

'Definitely. She's a fighter.'

DAY 14 – SUNDAY 20TH MARCH 2022.

We had been trying to visit Juno every day we could and for as long as possible. Today I had been to see her on my own as my partner was at work. It was the same time 3:30pm and we made it a regular thing for as long as she was at the vets.

When I arrived the lovely vet nurse took me around the back again to the ICU kennels. I felt this was easier for her as there was less of a walk down the corridor. She didn't have her coat on this time and to my shock, I could see every single bone in her body and when she was lying down her shoulder blades pierced through her skin. All she did was stay mostly in the same position the whole visit. She was still so weak, lying wearily on her soft comfy bed in the ICU kennel. She was all curled up but settled at last. I kneeled beside her and stroked her softly as she placed her head in my lap. All I could think is *how did this even happen, and why to Juno?*

Soon it was time to leave her again and head off back home. At least I knew Juno was being looked after very well with five-star treatment, she's worth it and deserves the best.

I didn't have much interaction online today as I was still taking it all in. So, my other dog and I just spent the rest of the day together watching the tv snuggled up trying to take my mind off everything and cheer myself up as I was feeling really depressed and alone.

At half 6 that evening, my partner text me: 'What did you get up to today?'

'Just went to see Juno,' I said, before sending her some photos.

'She is so scarily thin!' she exclaimed.

'I know.'

'Every time I see those photos, I just can't help but get so mad at the dog sitter!'

'Me too,' I agreed.

'You should send them these photos and ask if a dog had attacked her.'

'That's exactly what I plan on doing.'

DAY 15 – MONDAY 21ST MARCH 2022.

Today, I went to see Juno a bit earlier, around 2pm. This time she managed to sit up during the visit, which means she is getting stronger! She also wouldn't leave my side and placed herself onto my knee and I could feel every single bone and excess skin overlapping on my leg. She seemed a bit perkier.

The vet then suggested surgery options and said she could have her operation as soon as Wednesday! But they were saying that she could come home until her surgery. Although I was very excited about this news, I was also very apprehensive and worried about not being able to manage her at home just yet. They also mentioned a possible saving of her leg, as it seemed to be clean and free of infection. Where they would put metal work in her leg, but this had a lot more risk of complications and infections, and she wouldn't be able to bend her leg.

Later that afternoon, Juno's previous dog walker messaged me to ask how Juno was doing.

'She's getting there slowly,' I replied, 'The vets said she'll hopefully have her surgery on Wednesday. She wouldn't leave my side when I saw her earlier.' I then sent a photo of when I'd visited Juno that day, when she'd been leaning into and trying to sit on my knee. She was still so thin, all her bones were sticking out as she didn't have her coat on again, and she had a nasty graze along her back, around six inches long. The other photo I had sent was of Juno sitting on her bed at the vet, just looking so depressed with her wounded leg all bandaged up and her drip still inserted into her left front leg.

'Bloody hell,' they replied. 'Oh, I'm so glad she's still alive. What's the option you've gone for then? Amputation, is it? Will she be coming back to yours then or does she need to stay elsewhere? If you need help looking after her, PLEASE do not hesitate to contact me! Don't want anything like this happening again.

'Yes, amputation we think will be the quickest and least complex thing for her. I think she'll be coming back to ours after, but it will be difficult; our shift patterns aren't the best, and neither is our garden – we moved house a few months ago. Thank you, I will.'

'Where have you moved to?' they asked.

'Not that far from the train station.'

'Can neither of you take some leave to be with her? What is the postcode?'

'I could see what I can get sorted out, but healthcare isn't the best industry to be in; they don't seem to care,' I replied, before telling them my new postcode.

'Ok. Well, it's doable, and I'm over your way now and again, so if you need any help, just let me know.'

'Thank you,' I said, 'I will.'

'No worries. What's the damage on her head and back? Was she definitely hit by a car?'

'On her head, it looks like an animal attack – I'm thinking another dog possibly, which would make sense why she fled like she did. And someone did say she got hit by a car not far from the pub, but with the extent of all the damage, how would she manage to run all the way to the bridge over onto the railway tracks? It could have been a train, I don't know. I just wish I knew what had happened.'

I had been wondering about this a lot. So, as Juno had somehow by a miracle, managed to survive 10 days with apparently no food or water, I looked up: 'How long can a healthy dog go without eating?'

It said most healthy dogs can go up to five days, but only if the dog is drinking plenty of water. Some can go for up to seven days. I know each dog is different and bigger dogs would last longer, but either way, to me, ten days seemed incredible, I sent this information to my partner, saying, 'If she'd stayed where she was found for the whole ten days, with no food or water… Juno's a miracle dog!'

'Honestly makes me wonder if there is a god,' she replied.

In response, I sent her a photo of when I'd visited Juno that day and added, 'The vets said she can stay in with them until her operation (they wanted to send her home until she had her surgery but it just wasn't practical at the moment, and I told them I'd rather her be looked after at the vets), and they did suggest that her leg could be saved as it was healing up quite well – but it would be a bit more expensive nearer £9,000 and then there's a higher risk of complications.'

'Yeah, let's not put her in any more pain and suffering than she's already been through, and needs be,' she said, 'and we don't want to risk any more complications.' I agreed.

Just then, another admin from the missing dogs group sent me a message: 'Hi,' they started, 'I'm one of the coordinators with the missing dog group and I am also a Liaison Officer with the Association of Dog Boarders. I was delighted when Juno was found, and although she's not in the best shape now, I know with your love, care and attention she will soon be on the mend, and you will have her home with you where she should be. The reason I'm getting in touch is that Licensing Enforcement are interested in speaking to you regarding your experience. I have explained how traumatic the past two weeks have been for you and said that I'd be willing to pass this on to you, and if you wish to pursue it, then I can put you in touch with the right person. Feel free to drop me a message if you want me to explain anything to you in more detail and I'll be happy to do so. Sending lots of positive thoughts to your Juno. Best wishes.'

I immediately replied: 'Hi, yes, I would be interested in speaking to them. Juno is getting stronger each day and hopefully will be having her surgery on Wednesday.'

'Can I give you a quick call?' they asked.

'Yes, that's fine.'

So, we had a good chat on the phone, and they mentioned the possibility of taking the dog sitter to small claims court, but I was a bit unsure of that. They also had then sent me the contact details for the licensing enforcement officer.

Later, through text, I had told them as I was looking through past conversations with the dog sitter that I really don't think they went out looking for Juno at all and nothing had made any sense. I don't know why they didn't seem to care that much; they didn't even call me or try and contact me or my partner to say she'd gone missing! And I then sent over the conversation for the admin to try and decipher.

Once they'd read everything, they messaged me back: 'I absolutely agree – they didn't seem one bit upset, just carrying on with their daily things as usual. So, they have kids living there as well? They'd never have been able to get a license in that case – what breed did you say their dog was?'

'I don't really know their living situation to be honest,' I replied, 'and I've got a photo; I'll send it now.' So, I sent the photo, the very same one I had sent the admin from the drones for lost dogs' group – the photo featuring the dog sitter's dogs.

'Something must have happened to make her bolt. Dogs will have spats, but the injuries she has don't look like they are from a little spat. Poor, poor girl,' they messaged back.

'Yeah, and she hasn't got it in her to attack, so she would just flee if she was being attacked herself.'

'Bless her. She'll be back home with you in no time at all. I think if you contact the licensing officer whenever you're ready, they will do everything they can to help you.'

'Yeah,' I replied, sending a photo of Juno resting on my knee, 'She didn't move from that spot the whole time I was there visiting her at the vets. And I've emailed them now, thanks.'

'Love her. She's had a proper battering, the poor little girl.'

'Yes, I just wish I knew what had really happened,' I told them. 'Surely if she had gotten hit by a car and ended up with those injuries, she wouldn't have been able to run off as far as she did? Unless she had gotten hit by another car – or even a train? My little boy is missing his cuddle buddy.'

I then sent photos of both Juno and my other dog cuddling up together.

'Aww bless him. She'll be needing all his cuddles so best he saves them up.'

'Yes, he'll be so happy to see her.'

Once I'd finished exchanging messages, I then told my partner about this conversation.

'They also said that the person from the dog boarding licensing and council hasn't been able to get hold of the dog sitter and suggest we go to court – but said to take our time.'

I then quickly added, 'Don't text them or anything about what's happening. Just maybe ask when they're planning on coming over, as they said they would.'

Soon after, the admin from the group chat asked how Juno was doing. I messaged back, 'She's doing well. She just needs to rest and eat and drink plenty, which she's doing. And to get her strength up. I saw her yesterday.' And moreover, I sent a photo I'd taken the day before when I visited her at the vets.

'So very skinny!' the admin replied, 'but it's good she's eating and drinking. She will soon put weight on and get stronger.'

'Definitely, she's always looking for food when we go to visit her.'

My partner messaged the group chat a couple of hours later: 'Her frailty still upsets me a lot. The more I see the photos, the more rage I have for the dog sitter!'

'Understandable,' agreed the admin. 'Try to get more contact details, talk to the dog warden, and make sure they know what's happened.'
Later on, that afternoon I messaged the group chat: 'She was sitting on my lap when I went to see her today,' I said, sending the group three photos from my visit.

'Big comfort for her. I hear our other admin has spoken with you – they will give you good advice. Hope Juno will get a lot stronger now. Here to help however I can.' They offered.

That evening, I sent the other admin from the missing dogs group a message saying that the dog sitter was appearing to reply to my partner's messages, though I wasn't too sure if it was over text or online.

'I think they said to my partner that they've been busy, that they'll pay back the sitting fee and will pop over when they can. But I highly doubt that will happen!'

'Well, that's a start! Send the conversations over to me and I'll have a look tomorrow,' they replied. 'I'm off to bed now, I get up at 4am.'

Later that night, I messaged the admin from the drones for lost dogs' group with the photos I'd taken of Juno when I went to see her earlier that day and said Juno didn't leave my side and leaned into me.

'Oh, my dear god, that poor, poor girl,' they replied. 'That looks like a nasty gash on her back, I wonder how she got that. Bless her, I'm so happy to hear she's getting the best treatment. And that's so lovely to hear she was leaning into you, that is so lovely. Bless her.'

'I'm still in the process of getting the CCTV from the council,' I continued, 'but they haven't got back to me yet. She's a miracle dog. I was just looking up Google today that dogs can usually last just seven days without food or water, and she managed ten days!'

The admin pointed out that this statement wasn't quite right. 'As long as the dogs can get to water, they can go without food for a lot longer. I know of a dog that was trapped underground for 17 days and survived. They tend to lose a lot of body weight – you see the pictures of dogs who have been missing for weeks and they turn up super thin.'

'Ah I see, I don't know if Juno had any access to water or food though, plus all of her injuries would have made it much more difficult for her to survive, surely?'

'Yes, that gash on her back looks nasty, poor girl.'

'Do you think the gash could have been the result of being hit by some kind of vehicle – a car or train? I really want to know and wish I knew what had actually happened,' I told them.

'I honestly couldn't tell you.' They replied. 'Considering where she was found, it could have been a train – and she's tall enough to have been hit by the carriage itself. The poor girl has been in a right old battle, bless her. Those marks on her head look definitely like bites to me, and it's possible those are bite marks on her legs as well… if any dogs were onto her at the same time, she wouldn't have had a chance, poor thing.'

I had also sent an email soon after the contact with the other admin from the missing dogs' group to the licensing enforcement officer for our area: 'Hi, this is Juno's owner. An admin from a missing dogs group online has just contacted me, and I spoke on the phone to them, and they have passed on your information. I understand that you have tried to get hold of the dog sitter, with no luck. I've not managed to get in contact either, but I'm still quite angry at what their carelessness has done. On the other hand, I think my partner has been in contact with them but I'm not 100% sure. Juno is thankfully doing well; hopefully, she'll have her operation this Wednesday.'

Their reply came shortly after: 'Hi, thanks for getting in touch. I can only imagine how upsetting this has been for you, and I hope Juno is getting better. I have tried contacting them but with no success and it seems as if their online page has been taken down. As I have discussed with the admin who gave you my details, unless we can get an address for them, it will be very difficult for me to further my investigation, I would be most grateful. If you want to contact me, my mobile number is below.'

I then replied, 'They are back out walking dogs, so their page is now back up and running. I've messaged them with no reply, but I can do my best.' I then sent screenshots of previous conversations I'd had with the dog sitter.

Having looked back online, I knew they were still posting photos of dog walks all over their business page as if nothing had ever happened! How could anyone just carry on with their normal day-to-day routine when they had this in their conscience? Did they even have a conscience? I guess we'll never know…

DAY 16 – TUESDAY 22ND MARCH 2022.

Yesterday, I had messaged my sister's friend, who had been involved in a lot of missing dog cases and who had helped a lot when Juno had gone missing:

'Update on Juno: the vet says she can have her surgery on Wednesday! They did give me an option to save her leg, but it would be a lot more expensive, more complicated, and with a higher risk of infection and failure. So, we'll be sticking with the amputation. She sat on my knee for the duration of the visit earlier.' I then sent her some photos.

'Hiya, I was going to message you to ask how she was. Thank you. You know I was in tears when I first saw those photos. Your poor baby, what she's having to go through. So glad she's doing well. Can I post an update on the group page?' She asked.

She had created a group page online to help spread the word about Juno and to help with the GoFundMe page.

'I know, it's so upsetting.' I agreed.

Then I sent over the photos the rail workers had taken, when they first discovered her, and told her yes, she can post an update on the group page.

'Oh my god! So, she'd been like that since she went missing? Thank God the railway workers found her! I Bet she was so glad to see you both. She's a fighter. Thank you. So, was it definitely foxes and badgers that did those injuries?'

'I'm not entirely sure… it's all a bit sketchy and doesn't really add up. Foxes are hardly likely to attack a dog, they try to avoid conflict. Badgers too try to avoid any interactions, unless they feel threatened. I'm only assuming she may have been attacked by another dog due to where the injuries are and how bad they are.'

'Yes, it is all a bit strange, but could she have got to where she was found with those injuries?' she asked. 'What's happening with the dog sitter?'

'Maybe after the attack and car accident, she had an adrenaline rush that got her to the area she was last seen.' I suggested. 'Then maybe she just passed out with exhaustion and that was where she stayed, hidden, until the rail workers came and found her. The most frustrating thing is, my partner and I had walked past that same exact area every single day! But she didn't make any sound and we couldn't see her anywhere. The dog sitter has gone very quiet. I've had some news from others that they can't get hold of them and suggested I take things further.'

'Yeah, maybe, or I would've said she was dumped there?' She suggested.

I couldn't and wouldn't even fathom that this could have even been possible to happen to Juno. Someone had already suggested this on one of the online posts, and I'd had a full-on go at them – like how dare they suggest this when they don't know the full circumstances?! I just didn't want to believe this could be a possibility, it was such a sickening thought!

'Poor baby,' she continued, 'and it is a shame you couldn't find her before. I agree, don't let them get away with this! Are they even insured? They wouldn't go quiet if they had nothing to hide.'

'I don't know how likely it would be that she was dumped there,' I replied. 'I'm still trying to get CCTV from the council for the day she went missing. And no, they aren't insured. They said once their business sets off properly then they will sort it out. Maybe that's why they're hiding.'

'I hope you get the CCTV soon. They can be reported to the council. Let me speak with the police liaison at DogLost, if that's OK with you?'

'Yes, I'll keep following it up. And yes, that's fine with me, thank you. I did get a message from one of the coordinators of the missing dog's group – they had said someone is actively trying to get hold of them, but with no luck. They don't even know where they live…

They don't seem to want anyone to find them, or to even know the possible truth of what happened that day she went missing.'

'So, they pick up people's dogs and no one knows where they live? Doesn't sound at all right to me.

I'll see what help I can get from the police liaison officer.'

'Thank you so much!'

At 8:30 this morning, I messaged the admin from the drones for lost dogs' group: 'I've just received an email from the council,' I told them, 'Hopefully they will have looked into the CCTV and will have a response for me by the end of the day.'

'Brilliant,' they replied, 'let's hope that it shows something.'
I was wondering if maybe the CCTV could show whether Juno did in fact get hit by a car.

I soon then received a message from my sisters' friend: 'Hiya, how are you today? How is Juno? I'm waiting on the police liaison officer to get back to me.'

'Not bad thanks. I just got off the phone to the vets, she's doing good, and I'll be seeing her later today as they're going to be going ahead with her surgery tomorrow! Thanks, let me know if and when they get back to you. The council have got back to me about the CCTV just now too, they said I should hear something from them by the end of the day.'

'Glad you're OK, and I'm glad she's doing OK – give her an extra hug and kiss from me. That's good news, hopefully I'll hear back today as well. I'll let you know.'

I then phoned the vets up to ask when I could go and see Juno. They said this afternoon at around 5pm. I had always looked forward to these visits as I couldn't wait until she was back home for good and fully recovered.

Time just seemed to go so slow today, maybe it was because I was constantly thinking and worrying about Juno. But finally, it was time to get ready to go and see her, before her big day. This time the vet nurse took me through to one of the veterinary examination rooms where I was to sit and await Junos presence. She came limping in as the vet nurse placed the vet bed onto the floor for her. Laying on the comfy bed, I decided to lie down beside her and cuddle her. I told her she's going to have her operation tomorrow and that I knew she was going to be brave and how strong she is. I spent a good long hour with her before I decided to let her get some much-needed rest before her surgery.

At 7pm, I sent my sister's friend some photos of when I'd gone to see Juno earlier that day. Everyone was so grateful to me for sending them daily updates and photos of her.

'Aww poor baby, I pray all goes well tomorrow. It's truly heart breaking what she's had to suffer through.'

'Thank you. And I know – she's way too young to have gone through so much suffering already in her short little life.'

'Yes, I agree. And how scared she would have been too… it's upset me so much, and I know how much she means to you both. Your sister said Juno doesn't like being on her own?'

'Yes, we've had her nearly a year now,' I told her. 'We rescued her, and yes, she suffers from separation anxiety from being an unwanted lockdown puppy. Our other dog only grew out of it a few years ago when we could start leaving him to roam the whole house without doing anything, and he's now just over 6 years old. So, hopefully Juno will realise in time that it's OK to be left sometimes and that we'll always come back.'

'Poor baby, it takes time. Every dog is different, though it's now going to be much harder for her, after what she's been through,' she pointed out. 'Thank God again for those workers finding her when they did. I have a dog that also has separation anxiety, had him three years – got him free from an online selling site. My other one I've had 11 years now, he's OK.'

'Yes, I really want to quit my job or change career so I can be with her more,' I told her. 'My partner's nephew was living with us when we got her, so he was always there, but since he moved out – and we've moved house, she's just been a bit unsettled. But, hopefully, with a lot of work, time and patience, she'll get there. That's why we needed a dog sitter and walker in the first place, as we both work such long shifts.'

'It's hard when someone's around all the time and then they're not,' she agreed. 'You think they might be OK, but they're not. I can't go out much or for long at all. I hope you find something more suitable, and you can be with her more. She will need you both when she comes home. Any news on the dog sitter yet?'

'My ideal job would be to work from home, working on the frontline through the pandemic... I've still not really processed it all, and then this all happens with Juno... My mental health is at the breaking point right now, and I dread going into work. No news regarding the dog sitter – this is ridiculous!'

'That would be good, working from home,' she agreed. 'It's very hard, isn't it? Aww, I so feel for you, having to go through this on top of everything else. Oh my god, they should be facing up to this – not running off and hiding!'

'Yeah, it's really getting to me now. I just want to send them all the photos I have of her looking so skinny and with all her injuries and just block them!'

'I can't believe how they're behaving,' she replied. 'They should have helped and paid for her treatment. I hope someone catches up with them!' She then sent me a screenshot of another missing dog around the area where we live.

'I hope so too. And aww no, why are there so many dogs going missing recently?' I asked.

'It's gone mad, all these dogs are going missing. I'm doing the listings on the group this week – it's non-stop.'

'Makes me never want to leave Juno and my other dogs' sides ever again.'

'I know what you mean – since the pandemic, it's gone crazy. I'm scared to even walk mine... luckily, I have a green area right outside my house.'

'Same here. I've been reluctant to walk my other dog, as he's a very sought after breed, and you never know what can happen,' I replied. 'At least he's lazy and content; he loves nothing more than to sleep most – if not all – of the day, but he does love a good walk. The dog sitter tried to offer to walk him too, and as I've had him for so long, my bond is so strong with him and I'm way overprotective of him. I told the dog sitter that he's fine just sleeping on the sofa all day, but Juno can't do that; she needs the mental stimulation.'

'Yes, I guess they're worth a lot more money, and so many dogs are stolen. Good job they didn't look after him too.'

'Especially if they were looking after both Juno and my other dog,' I pointed out. 'If any dog was around that may have attacked Juno, my poor other dog wouldn't have stood a chance.'

'Thank God. How long had she been going to the dog sitter?' She asked.

'Walking since December, and only recently in the past month or so, had been sitting her.'

'Oh, OK. And yeah, maybe there was a dog that didn't like her or a dog she didn't like or was scared.'

'I'm thinking, because she's a lurcher, she can play quite rough sometimes,' I explained. 'Or the dog may have snapped back and attacked, and she bolted.'

'There are a lot of injuries she's got, and she doesn't seem like the kind of dog to attack anyone or anything.'

'Yes, she hasn't got it in her,' I agreed, 'she's just the sweetest dog you'll ever meet; everyone who has ever met her will agree.'

'Good luck for tomorrow,' she wished. 'I'll be thinking and praying for her.'

'Thank you,' I replied, 'so will we, and we will keep you updated.'

So, tonight was the night before Juno goes for her surgery, I couldn't stop worrying about all the things that could possibly happen whilst she would be under anesthetic. What if she bleeds out and they can't stop it? What if her body can't take it and just shuts down?

I just needed to get to sleep and try and take my mind off all the negatives.

DAY 17 – WEDNESDAY 23RD MARCH 2022.

Today was the day of Juno's lifechanging surgery. I was riddled with so many nerves and so much worry. Many questions are racing through my mind; *What if it's not successful? What if she has a reaction to the anesthetic and doesn't wake up?*

Not long after waking up, I phoned the vets to check if Juno was definitely going to have her surgery today, they replied and said that she was as she's at a healthy enough weight to deal with the anesthetic. The relief I felt was that the vets knew she was going to be strong enough to pull through.

That morning, after I had phoned the vets, I messaged the missing dogs group coordinator and sent a screenshot of the dog sitter's online page – the page where they were still actively posting photos of walking other people's dogs.

'That's a disgrace,' they replied. 'Unfortunately, the enforcement team can only deal with boarding issues, not walking. I bet they don't even have any business insurance!'

'But they boarded Juno! I don't think they do either. I just want to send every single photo that's been taken of Juno so far since she's been found to their personal inbox – I don't even think they've seen the full extent of her injuries.'

'Write a review on their page,' they suggested, 'They can't dispute it – it's all fact.'

I then sent them a screenshot of what I'd just messaged the dog sitter. 'I've sent this… But I don't really want to see the reply.'

'Good on you! They need to take some if not all responsibility.'

The coordinator then sent me a screenshot of the review I had written on their page two months earlier; I was the first one to put a review! When they first started out and started walking Juno. It read:

'Is dependable and extremely helpful, is a great laugh and I don't think we would want anyone else to walk our dog! We recommend if you need a dog walker, trustworthy and hard-working!' They then told me to edit my review.

'Well,' I swallowed hard and said, 'two months ago, this did apply.'

'I'm sure it did. But you know better now – they're clueless and dangerous.'

'And once Juno comes back home, she's going to need 24-hour care and support,' I informed. 'She'll need to be fed every few hours. I just want to quit my job right now.'

'Bless you. It's an absolute nightmare for you, which is why I want to do whatever I can to help,' they offered.

'Thank you,' I replied.

At 9:40am, I had sent the dog sitter the most graphic and real photos I could find of what happened to Juno – what would it take for them to realise what they had done?! They needed to see them – to know what their negligence had done. It started off, 'Do you not care??' and then to await their reply.

The dog sitter didn't reply until almost 6pm that evening, stating they had family over so couldn't reply and that they had also only just got in from work. Asking to come over another day still! Then the attitude that came out of them. I shook my head whilst reading the feeble excuses, and saying they did everything they could the day she went missing – sure, they did everything... except for telling us as soon as she'd run away! I wasn't accusing their dogs of attacking Juno; but when that subject came up, they went full-on aggressive and saying how their dogs had never attacked before and that they were the best-behaved dogs. Maybe they were. I shook my head again; even the best-behaved dog could snap and attack... how naive they were to simple dog behaviour. They then said they'd be over now with Juno's lead and name tag.

I couldn't believe this message. After all, all I'd done was ask if it could've been a slight possibility for their dogs to have had a bit of a tiff with Juno if she was playing too rough or something and they may have attacked her; I didn't know where they'd got the idea that I was fully accusing them and that they'd done it on purpose!? Their attitude was very unpleasant, and if they had nothing to hide, they surely wouldn't have replied to the way they did, surely? I didn't really want anything more to do with them after this point, so I just sent more photos. I didn't need this, especially when this was the day Juno was having her major operation. They then stated that they were no coward and would tell me if their dogs had attacked Juno – but didn't tell us when she ran way...

I eventually replied:

'My mental health has been vastly affected by all of this; I'm even considering going off sick long-term from work. I've worked on a covid ward all throughout the pandemic and I still haven't quite processed it all, and now this happens. I'm done. I'm not saying your dog attacked her or you did this on purpose – maybe they had a bit of a scrap in the garden and maybe that's why Juno fled. I'm not accusing you. And she's had to have her back amputated today!'

They then replied, not mentioning asking how Juno was or how sorry they were, just kept on defending their dogs.

I didn't reply; I didn't want to talk to them anymore.

Soon after I received a phone call from the vets. They had said the surgery was a success! Everything was going so well, and I asked if it would be possible for me to come and see her in the morning and they said I could once they updated me on her condition if she was well enough for me to come and see her.

At 6:30pm, I sent a screenshot of this conversation to the coordinator of the missing dogs group.

'And not one hint of an apology?!' they replied.

'Yeah, I just don't know what to say anymore,' I told them, before adding, 'update on Juno: she has had her surgery and it all went well! Hopefully I can go and see her in the morning.'

'Ah bless her. She'll come on in leaps and bounds, guaranteed. They adapt so quickly. Let me know how she's doing please. Have you thought about getting legal advice to sue the dog sitter for ongoing costs?'

'Yeah, she will,' I agreed, 'and will do. And I'm not sure about it yet, it may be more hassle than it's worth.'

Just before 7pm, I messaged my sister's friend: 'Update on Juno, she has now had her surgery and is doing well. She now just needs to be monitored overnight and I'll hopefully be seeing her in the morning.'

'Wow, that's fantastic news!' she replied. 'Thank God it went well. Bet you can't wait until then?'

'Yeah, I'm so glad,' I agreed, 'and I can't wait to see her tomorrow. Hopefully, she'll be home by the weekend.'

DAY 18 – THURSDAY 24TH MARCH 2022.

Today was the day we would go to visit Juno post-op. I was feeling so overwhelmed and apprehensive and trying to prepare myself as to what I was going to see – but nothing could be as bad as how Juno looked when she was first found, could it?

I'd called the vets to arrange a time to visit her, and they had told me we could come and see her at around 10am.

Soon it was time to get ready and prepare us for our visit to see Juno. We jumped straight into the car, and I drove nervously to the veterinarian hospital not knowing what Juno would look like.

Once we arrived, we sat down in the waiting area, the vet nurse soon called us to come into a separate room. It was called the 'family room.' Once stepping inside this room, I could soon tell that this was the room where they put pets to sleep… Looking around and I saw a jar of chocolates which had printed on it, 'every dog deserves to taste chocolate before they go to heaven' – I then started to well up by just reading this. I Then took a deep breath and sat down on the sofa they had available, next to my partner.

The anticipation was driving me crazy.

Soon, we heard the pitter-patter of paw-steps coming down the corridor, and as the door opened Juno's little sad face appeared, I nearly started to cry again and as the vet nurse brought out a soft bed for her to comfortably lie on whilst she spent the time with us. The vets were ever so surprised with Juno and how she was doing; they told us that they thought Juno would need help and struggle getting herself up out of the ICU kennel to come and see us – but no – they said she got straight up! We knew from the start that she was a fighter! The vet nurse then left us to it and spend some much-needed time with Juno.

Juno had part of her tail removed and had a white bandage wrapped around it – she had to have half of her tail amputated as well as her leg, as it was so damaged her tail bone was sticking out through the skin. She looked like a patchwork doll with many areas of her fur shaved off, due to the number of injuries she had sustained all over her body.

The amputation was a massive shock, but the incision looked so neat and tidy. She looked so sad and defeated, but with a hint of relief that she must have felt that her painful leg had now been taken off.

I then lay on the floor next to her and cuddled into her for a good long while.

Soon it was time for us to go, as Juno was starting to look like she was in pain and needed some well-earned rest. I hugged and kissed her goodbye and told her we'll be back to see her soon.

Then the nurse came to collect Juno and she stood up stiffly and hobbled following the vet nurse back to her ICU kennel where she would now be given some more pain relief and some food.

It was such a heart wrenching sight to witness for us, but to know she was being looked after so well and was well on the way to recovery gave me great comfort.

When we got back from the vets, I sent some photos of a post-op Juno to my sisters' friend.

'Thank god she's doing well,' she quickly replied, 'but I'm gutted she had to lose her leg. Can I update the group?'

'Yes, it is a shame she had to,' I agreed, 'but I'm sure she'll do really well on three legs.'

'Yes, she will get used to it, poor baby. At least she has you, your partner, and your other dog to give her lots of love, care and support.

Have they given you a date when she can come home?'

'No, not yet, but hopefully after the weekend.'

At around 2pm that day, the coordinator from the missing dog's group had sent me an interesting link online. It was a post from one of the content researchers from a big TV company. They were looking for people who'd had good and bad experiences with dog boarders.

'That would be one in the eye for the dog sitter!' they said.

'Definitely,' I sent back, before immediately replying to the online post with all the details about what happened to Juno whilst staying with her dog sitter. I also sent some photos from the most recent visit to the vets.

I then also sent the coordinators some photos from when I'd gone to see Juno earlier after her operation. 'I saw her today,' I told them. 'She's doing really well, bless her.'

I had sent some photos of Juno standing up on her now three legs.

'Look at her up and about! She is one little toughie! Fair play to her! You know,' they added, 'I reckon the TV program would run with your story. The trauma, and then how the community and further got behind you with the crowdfunding.'

'Yes, that would be so good,' I agreed. 'I've messaged the content researcher about Juno. When I saw her earlier, the vet nurses thought that she would need extra help getting up from lying down in her ICU kennel, but they said she did really well on her own and surprised them all!'

'She is incredible!'

'She is!' I agreed.

Later that day, the admin from the drones for lost dogs group messaged me: 'Hi, is there any news on Juno? Has she had her operation? How is she doing?'

'Hi, yes, she's doing amazingly well already on her three legs!' I replied, before sending them some photos.

'Aww my god, bless her, I think somebody is peeling onions in my house.'

'Aww.'

'I'll put these pictures up on the post now, unless you want to do it to update the post?'

'You can put the photos up, thank you!'

'Will do,' they replied. Then continued, 'the more I look at Juno's injuries, the more I'm convinced she was attacked. She may have been bumped by the car as well, but I don't think all those injuries were caused by a car. Please don't ever let her stay at that dog sitters house again. If a dog did cause these injuries, it's not worth the risk.'

'Don't worry, I won't ever be doing that again,' I told them. 'The dog sitter got extremely defensive when I mentioned it and asked about it.' I then sent the screenshots of the conversation over.

'They don't seem to understand that it may have been a bit of a scrap between Juno and another dog – or dogs – and may have gone a bit too far. Also, they said that if anything like that did happen, they would've got proper treatment for her… but she ran away…'

'Yes, but did she run away after the possible attack, and they didn't know what had happened?'

'Yes, maybe. That's what I was thinking.' I then sent the image of Juno's last sighting at the railway. 'I wish I could see this photo in better quality. It's hard to see her back leg, to see if it was at all disfigured at that point.'

'Yes, it is hard to see,' they agreed, 'but by the way she's standing, there are no obvious injuries.'

'But' looking harder at the picture, 'her right back leg looks a bit out of place to me, don't you think? Which is the same leg that had to be amputated.'

'I think that may just be the way she's standing,' they pointed out, 'as if she'd come to a stop mid-run.'

I then had found some older photos on my phone of Juno on one of our walks – where she was standing up – and sent them over. 'It's hard to tell.'

'Yes, I think it really is just the way she's standing, it's very similar to the older picture. She's lost part of her tail as well, hasn't she?'

'Yes,' I replied, before sending them the photo of Juno's damaged tail – bone sticking out at the tip.

'Dear, dear, dear, what the hell are all these injuries? I can't begin to imagine what she must have gone through to get all these injuries. Poor, poor girl.'

'I wish I knew; I wish she could tell me. The council say they've got nothing on their CCTV footage for that day, but maybe it had already been deleted.'

'Yes, probably.'

At 7pm, I sent an update to the admin of the missing dog's group, saying how she was doing – really well – along with some recent photos of Juno at the vets.

'Very glad to hear that, I've been thinking about her a lot. You may get a message from a woman; it will be worth having a chat with her. She helped with organising the recovery of a dog that was involved in a traffic accident – she may have some good tips to help, so please watch out for any messages. So glad to see Juno doing so well.'

'Thank you. I will do.'

I never did get a message from the woman, unless it went into my junk folder, but I never did find anything.

Then at around 10pm, I sent Juno's previous dog walker the photos of her that I'd taken earlier that day whilst we visited her a day after her operation.

'Oh, bless her,' they replied. 'Are you both OK?'

'I'm going to need to start thinking about getting a month or so off sick from work,' I explained. 'My mental health has reached the point where I know that, if I were to carry on working, I'd do something stupid. She's doing well with three legs – the vets were really amazed by her, how she got up so easily from lying down – and I know she's going to come back from this like a boss! I'll hopefully have her back home after the weekend. I'll send you my most recent messages between the dog sitter and

I; I feel so confused and conflicted.'

After I'd sent over the screenshots of the conversation, they replied, 'Absolutely, mate. Take the time you need with her. She'll be a boss and she'll get through this in no time. Just be as patient as you can with her. It's not going to be easy. I've worked with a three-legged dog before and rehabilitated them, and it's going to be so worth it! I promise you that. Just glad she is here. As for the dog sitter… I don't like their attitude with it all, to be honest.'

'That's why I'm not bothering to argue,' I replied. 'I'm just going to be sending them nothing but photos to hopefully send the message of what has actually happened, hopefully soon they'll come to some kind of realisation.'

'I hope you get some answers,' they said. 'If you don't, then it's just best to stay away – focus on Juno and make sure people are aware. I've seen that the business page is back up and running…'

'Yes, that really annoyed me when I had seen it was back up.'

'Complete arrogance.'

I couldn't agree more.

DAY 19 – FRIDAY 25TH MARCH 2022.

At around 10am, I sent an email to the content researcher for the TV program as they had requested, I also spoke on the phone with them and explained everything in more detail that had happened with the situation and Juno.

Then, at around 11:30am, my sister's friend messaged me:

'Hey, hope you're all good. How's Juno doing today?'

I had been on the phone to the vets first thing at 9am for an update.

'Hopefully she will be coming home today!' – She was recovering so well! – I replied, before telling her all about the TV program wanting to do Juno's story.

'That's really good news to hear. Wow, she is going to be so popular... though she is already! Have you heard from the story the director of the railways had done?' she asked.

'No, but I've been in contact with them and emailing them with updates.'

'That's good, are they doing the story?'

'I'm not too sure about that.'

At lunchtime, I had messaged the admin from the drones for lost dogs, telling them all about the TV people were interested in doing Juno's story and I had been in contact with them. I was keeping the news about Juno a secret for the moment as we were still not 100% if she was coming home today.

I also messaged the admin from the missing dogs' group about being on TV – how they were interested in doing Juno's story.

'Are you going to do it?' they asked.

'Yes, I think so.'

'That's great, you never know what help might come from it – hopefully, it will also help, so that this sort of thing doesn't ever happen again.'

'Yes, definitely,' I agreed.

At around 3pm, my partner and I were then on our way to pick Juno up from the vets!

She was finally coming home!

Arriving at the hospital full of nerves and anticipation, worrying about how we were going to look after her. Once we got there, the vets sat us down and told us some strict instructions and gave us a leaflet which was titled:

'Post leg amputation care', and read:

At home keep Juno in a **WARM**, **QUIET** and **COMFORTABLE** environment.

•   <u>Feeding</u> – Please follow the feeding plan provided.

•   <u>Walking</u> – Lead walks **ONLY** for at least 14 days. Ensure the walks are no longer than 10 minutes at a time. If Juno is reluctant to walk, please **DO NOT** encourage her, as this may be a sign of pain – please let us know as soon as possible so we can get some extra pain relief.

•   <u>Cryotherapy</u> – (Cryotherapy is the use of placing an extreme cold object, for example an ice pack, onto the affected area to freeze abnormal tissue and help reduce swelling). Please perform cryotherapy on the stump three times a day. Cryotherapy should not last any longer than 15 minutes and if Juno seems uncomfortable at any point please stop and try again later. Please ensure you cover the ice pack with the J – cloth provided and that the ice pack does not go directly onto Juno's skin.

•   <u>Wounds</u> – Please monitor the wounds for any signs of infection, including discharge and foul odour. If there is any excessive bleeding, please call us as soon as possible.

•   <u>Physiotherapy</u> – If you would like to book Juno in for physiotherapy, please let the reception team know.

Then on the same leaflet, it said about her medications.

MEDICATION

Juno has two forms of pain relief to go home with – **LOXICOM** and **PARDALE** – (Loxicom is used to relieve inflammation and pain in cats and dogs. It can be used for acute – sudden and short-lived-musculoskeletal disorders, for example, due to injury or surgery. Pardale is used as a pain relief mainly in dogs. It is also used for acute pain of traumatic origin, to use with and alongside other pain relief due to a range of conditions and post operative pain.

LOXICOM – Please give a 17.5mg dose ONCE daily. Please give this after food. **STOP GIVING THIS MEDICATION IF THERE IS ANY VOMMITING AND DIARRHOEA.** Please start – 8am, 26/03/2022.

PARDALE – Please give **HALF** a tablet twice daily. Please start – 8pm on 25/03/2022.

If you feel Juno is still uncomfortable, please let us know as we can add additional pain relief.

ANTIBIOTIC – Please continue the course as stated on the box until ALL tablets have been used.

NOROCLAV - Give one tablet, twice daily. Please start – 8pm on 25/03/2022

Please feel free to call with any questions you may have.

We had also been given a strict feeding plan for Juno:

- **IMPORTANT** – Please follow this feeding plan so we know the extent of any weight loss or gain.

• **FOOD** – Specific intensive support.
Juno will need 3 cans a day in total. **PLEASE FEED** 237g **PER FEED**
(Just under 2/3 of the can.)

• A rest period between 10pm and 6am is needed.

• If any additional food is fed, please note it on this food diary and
include the calorie content.

We were to follow this food diary over the course of the weekend and
the vets had filled out the first three boxes on the chart for today.

Friday 25th March 2022; 6am – 237g 100% eaten, 10am – 237g
100% eaten, 2pm – 237g 100% eaten. Her next feeding time was due at
6pm.

So, as the vet nurse was on their way to get Juno, we sat in the waiting
room, waiting to pick Juno up, I was filled with excitement to finally have
her back.

She came limping into the room and the excitement on her face was
priceless, she came straight over to my partner and I with her little stub of a
tail briskly wagging. Then it was soon time to take her home.

We walked her slowly to the car – one of us carrying the food and medication, the other holding her lead. Once we had got to the car, I gently lifted her up trying not to touch or knock her amputation site in the process and placed her safely into the car with my partner in the back with her.

Then we were off back home!

Upon bringing Juno home, our other dog was so happy to see her and kept giving her kisses, but we had to keep both of them calm.

I had bought a special veterinary bed just for her to have something comfortable and soft to lie on – although she soon managed to worm her way up onto the sofa, her favourite place.

At just past 5pm, after I had brought Juno back from the vets, my partner had sent a photo to the group chat of her and Juno in the back seat of the car.

'Is she going home?' they replied, a while later.

In response, I sent a photo of her lying on her vet bed along with the caption: 'She's home!'

'Bless her, she must be so pleased to be home.

Being home will help with her recovery now, she will rest much better.'

'Definitely.'

I had then messaged to let Juno's old dog walker, 'She's back where she belongs!' along with a few photos.

'Aww bless her,' they replied. 'Glad she's home now.'

Then, at 6:10pm, after we had fed Juno and she was settled, I sent my sisters' friend a photo of Juno, finally at home!

'Aww, how is she?'

'She seems settled and very drowsy. Just chilled out and relaxed,' I replied.

'Aww, so happy she's doing well. I will update the group.'

'Thank you.'

I soon sent a message to the admin from the drones for lost dogs' group:

'She's back where she belongs!' followed by three photos: One of her lying on her vet bed, one of her relaxing on the sofa, and one with my other dog kissing her.

'Aww bless her, this is so good to see,' they replied.

'Our other dog, although he is happy, she's back, he is acting like a moody little child now.' I jokingly said as I sent them a photo of him sulking.

'Ha ha ha.'

'He'll stay there now, just sulking. Told him off once to be careful around Juno, and he literally went to the other side of the room and just sat there, staring at the wall for half an hour.'

'Ha ha ha. Bloody hell.'

'He is such a baby at times.' I laughed to myself.

That evening and night was very tough, we had to feed Juno again at 10pm after her 6pm feed, also remembering to give her medication. We wrote in her food diary that the vets had given us, and she never left a single morsel of food.

When it came to letting her out to do her business, I had to carry her up our steps in the back garden as she couldn't go up steps just yet – I was kind of glad she wasn't too heavy, as this felt like a workout in itself.

Then we were all ready for bed after a very busy day, we fell asleep on the sofa for the rest of the night.

DAY 20 – SATURDAY 26TH MARCH 2022.

I had an early start this morning as I had to feed Juno at 6am, give her medication and take her out into the garden carrying her up the steps out to do her business.

At 10am I messaged the coordinator for the missing dogs group.

'I've just had someone message me about the dog sitter, they had come to the conclusion that the dog sitter had been way overcharging for the sittings!' I was in the same position; they were taking advantage of desperate dog owners. They want to know if there's a possibility of suing or getting most of the money back, as they're still out there walking dogs so still earning money, probably even more than myself!'

'How much were they charging?'

I embarrassingly and deflatingly replied to the exact amount.

'Per night??'

'Yes. And I remember that my old dog sitters, who were licensed and insured, only charged a fraction of that amount!'

'That's a joke', they replied. 'We've been in business eight years and only charge a bit less than your old dog sitters per day. They've taken you and others for an absolute ride, to be honest. There's nothing you can do about what they've already charged, unfortunately, as it's their fee. But I think I would probably take legal advice from Citizens Advice, or with a no win no fee firm (they would take a cut of any win, though). What has the contact at licensing said?'

'They just said to proceed, they need an address.'

'Which we can't get.'

'I'll try my best to get the address. I've also noticed, strangely how their business page keeps going down and then back up again,' I pointed out.

'Getting new clients every day by the looks of it too,' they replied.

'Until they start getting some honest reviews, they'll just carry on taking on more dogs and putting them all at risk.'

'What would it take in order for them to realise what they've done?' I asked.

They then told me that hopefully karma will catch up to them.

I tried asking Citizens Advice but got nowhere.

A few minutes later, I sent my sister's friend a photo of my other dog and Juno sleeping next to each other lovingly.

'Morning,' she replied. 'I was just going to message you. Aww, so glad that she is home now and safe, well looked after and with plenty of TLC.'

'Definitely.'

'I still get so tearful about what she's been through,' she added. 'So glad everything went well, and she will go on to live a happy and healthy life.'

Then, later that evening, she messaged again, asking how Juno was doing.

'She's doing well,' I replied and sent an updated photo. 'Hard work; we must feed her a certain amount of food each day at 6am, 10am, 2pm and 10pm. And taking her out to the toilet is a bit of a workout – we must carry her up our steep steps into our garden as she can't walk upstairs yet, at least she's not too heavy – and all the medications we must give her at certain times.'

'Aww yeah, but so worth it. So happy to hear, and the photo is so cute. When is she going for her check-up?'

'Definitely. And her check-up is on Monday.'

'That's good, I'm sure they'll be happy with her progress over the weekend.'

'Yes, she seems to be putting on weight well so far.'

'That's fantastic! She'll soon be back to herself again.'

'Certainly. I'm going to be taking some time off sick from work as it's all gotten too much, and I can't be expected to look after Juno whilst I'm at work on a 12-hour shift.'

'That's good, it's what she needs right now. What about after?'

'We'll get to that when the time comes; I'm reducing my hours at work anyway.'

'Good.' She said then the conversation ended.

I had spent the day keeping a close eye on Juno and making sure she was eating and drinking with no issues and checking the wounds for any sign of infection. She seemed to be slowly getting her spark back and seemed happier and more settled in herself.

I know it won't take long for this strong girl to get back to normal.

.

DAY 21 – SUNADY 27TH MARCH 2022.

When I awoke this morning, I was just fixated on Juno, looking at her sleeping and appreciating every second that she was still here with us.

That morning I was feeding Juno, watching her lap up every single drop of her food and licked the bowl extra clean. Then time for her medications which made her drowsy for the day.

My sister's friend messaged me at lunchtime. 'Hiya, hope you're all well. How is Juno doing today?'

'She's doing really well, thanks,' I responded, sending her yet another photo of Juno, but this time wrapped up in a blanket looking all cozy, relaxed and comfy.

'Aww how cute! I'm so, so happy she's doing so well.'

'Our other dog is getting super jealous, though,' I told her, 'He's acting like a spoilt little child!'

'Aww, she just needs you more now.

Did you get the money straight away from the funding? As I'm having problems with the one that I'm doing with my friend.'

'It takes a while,' I agreed. 'We did have some issues at the beginning.'

'Ah, OK.

Hopefully she can get the money out tomorrow – though we need to raise more.'

'We did ours on Thursday 17th March,' I informed her, 'and we started getting it processed straight away. I had to scrape the first £1,000 together myself for the next day though, as the vets demanded it. Then, I think, around Tuesday 22nd March or Wednesday 23rd March, it came through.

I hope your friend can get the money out soon.'

'I hope so too; we're trying. Glad you managed to get the first lot of money together.'

'Yes, it was literally all I had and basically my whole month's wage. I do hope so.'

I then told her how well Juno was doing with eating, drinking and walking.

'Oh wow. I'm so glad she's doing so well,' she replied. 'I love getting these updates.'

Later, we took Juno out for a small 10-minute walk like the vets had suggested. We put a little coat on her to stop her from getting cold and to cover up how bony and skinny she still was. We let her take her time and have a few good sniffs around. Many people stopped us in the street and asked us what had happened, and as we explained they wished Juno a very speedy recovery.

DAY 22 – MONDAY 28TH MARCH 2022.

That morning, I sent the admin from the missing dogs group another photo of Juno.

'Aww bless her, how is she doing?' they asked.

'She's doing very well, thank you.'

'That's great. She looks a lot happier; she's clearly glad to be home.'

'Most certainly,' I agreed. 'Our other dog is being a pain in the bum though – he's acting like a spoilt child.'

'Ha, attention seeking.'

'Yes, he had jumped up at me to sit on my knee earlier, even though he didn't look one bit comfortable at all.'

Juno went for her check-up today, they had weighed her and said she had lost a little bit of weight which made me feel quite disappointed in myself. Did I make her lose that weight? The vet then reassured me that it happens, especially with refeeding. Other than that, she was doing pretty well with everything else, they did a few tests as well. They told us to now up her food, so she was consuming a few more calories daily, we were also giving her a few Bonio biscuits throughout the day.

A bit later, my sister's friend messaged me: 'Morning, I hope the vet visit went well today.'

'She's lost a bit of weight which I'm disappointed at,' I told her, 'So they've upped her food now and given us plenty more cans. She's now going to be on 1 full can every four hours.'

'Aww, but is everything else OK for now?'

'Hopefully. She's got another check-up on Wednesday.'

'Ah, OK.

Have you got a recent photo of Juno to update the group with please?'

'Yes, I'll send one over now.' I then sent her a photo of Juno when she'd just come back from the vets, with two little green bandages around her front legs. 'She had to have a blood test to check if everything was all OK.'

'Thank you. Aww, so cute. The members of the group look forward to her updates.'

I then sent her a screenshot of a post I'd seen online. It was about a campaign in Wales to stop greyhound racing, and the picture on the post showed three, three-legged greyhounds – all with one of their back legs missing. 'Aww. I saw this post online earlier – it's sad how a lot of greyhounds get their injuries from racing.'

'I had seen this post yesterday,' she replied, 'and yes, it's horrible. There are a few greyhounds and lurchers in my local rescue center.'

'It is horrible and sickening – animal cruelty,' I agreed, before adding light heartedly, 'but this is Juno's crew now!'

DAY 23 – TUESDAY 29TH MARCH 2022.

Rather worryingly that day, after doing the morning routine of toilet, food and medication, we had spotted some blood on Juno's blanket she had been lying on. It was then starting to become a bit more heavier and alarming, when she would walk around, blood would be dripping constantly wherever she went leaving a trail of blood behind her.

We went straight to our phone and immediately called the vets, as we remember reading on the leaflet that if she starts to bleed, call the vets straight away. We then had to take her back to the vets. As she had now started to bleed quite heavily from her amputation site, she had to stay there for a few hours and was given special medication to help slow the bleeding. The vet also reassured us that it's usually very common for lurchers and greyhound-type dogs to have issues with bleeding. The vets had placed a big dressing wrapped around her stump to absorb the bleeding.

There she had to stay to get her bleeding under control and sorted.

Then, at 12:30pm, Juno's old dog walker messaged me: 'How is she doing, buddy?'

'She had a bit of bleeding from her amputation site, so we had to pop her back to the vets,' I explained. 'And she's now there until a bit later, as they've now put her on a new medication to help clot her blood. But she's gained 600g!'

'Aww, no! I hope it's not too bad. Ah, that weight gain is brilliant, at least she's got some more weight on her now and getting there steadily. Hope she's doing OK, yourself and your partner also.

Glad to hear she's getting there, slowly but surely.'

'Yes, I was so relieved when they said about her weight. She's doing well, sleeping on the sofa with me at night and being treated like a princess. I'm now taking time off work to make sure she's OK. I was supposed to be at work today, and my partner isn't driving. If I hadn't taken this time off, I can't imagine what would've happened today if I wasn't there! I don't know how my partner would've got Juno to the vets.'

'Hey, some things just happen for a reason,' they reassured, 'maybe this is the universe's way of telling you to slow down – take some time for yourself and focus on what's really important right now.'

'Yes, I do think so too.'

Then, my sister's friend messaged me to check on how Juno was doing. I told her about the bleeding and the slight weight gain and sent her a photo of the new dressing she had now wrapped around her amputation site, as well as a photo of Juno sleeping on the sofa. She promised to update the group with the photos, and I told her I'd be picking Juno up from the vets at 9pm that night.

We picked Juno up at 9pm and she looked so much better for it. She loved going to see the vets, she would always try and push the door open to where her ICU kennel was, and she knew where the vets kept the treats.

That night, I could hardly sleep as I was keeping a close eye on Juno and her bleeding. The blood was already coming through the dressings, but she was due to be seen tomorrow and she was on these new tablets to help stop the bleeding. We were using puppy pads to stop her from soiling the sofa with her blood.

DAY 24 – WEDNESDAY 30TH MARCH 2022.

I couldn't wait for the vet visit today, as Juno had bled a considerable amount of blood and her dressing so desperately needed to be changed. Once we arrived at the vets, they soon called Juno for her dressing change. Juno jumped all over the place, slipping and sliding and of course forgetting that she had just recently had surgery and only had three legs! Off she trotted with the vet nurse into the back room to get sorted. Soon she came back out with a nice fresh dressing around her amputation site, and we thanked them and off we went back home to have a good rest.

Later that day, the shooting director for the TV program sent me an email to introduce themselves and told me a bit about what happens and what's involved in taking part in doing the filming. They suggested it would be good to have a quick chat at some point today.

'Also, just to let you know,' they announced, 'we have had some issues with presenter availability, so we are looking at filming this next Friday now, 8th April. Is this OK with you?'

I replied: 'Hi, I've been very busy today with Juno at the vets – she's now got a fistula at the amputation site. That's fine with me. Thank you.'

I then spoke for quite some time on the phone with them and told them everything. They suggested I send them some photos of Juno before she went missing, when she was found, and after the amputation, which I did soon after the phone call.

That afternoon, I sent a message to the admin for the missing dogs group: 'Just an update on Juno: She's got some bleeding from her amputation site, so we've been going to the vets every day this week so far.' I also sent them a photo of Juno lying on her back, relaxing with her dressing around her stump, I loved how she didn't seem to be at all bothered by the bleeding. Such a strong girl!

'Aww, I hope it's not too bad,' they replied. 'Have the vets said anything?'

'Yesterday they said that, because she's a lurcher, they do tend to have a higher risk of bleeding, so they gave her some new medication to help with blood clotting. She had to stay at the vet yesterday evening. I hope she doesn't have to stay in again tonight.'

'I hope not – let's hope it's stopped, and she can stay home.'

At around the same time, I messaged the admin from drones for lost dogs: 'Update on Juno, she has started bleeding from her surgery site on her stump. So, we've been to the vets every day this week.'

And I sent them the same photos as the admin from the missing dogs group.

'Aww bless, is it an infection?' they asked. 'I'm sure they'll be able to sort it out with medication.'

'They said it's an internal pool of blood that had collected under the skin on the amputation site, and it just needed to escape from somewhere, so it made a fistula hole but now won't seem to stop bleeding,' I explained. 'She's now on new medication to help with blood clotting, as apparently the vet said lurchers and greyhounds are known to bleed heavily.'

'Aww bless,' they said, 'I'm sure she'll be OK. They know what they're doing, and she is in the best possible place for her, should she need to stay in.'

'Absolutely,' I agreed.

DAY 25 – THURSDAY 31ST MARCH 2022.

That day, the shooting director from the TV program had sent me some consent forms and asked me to send over our address.

'Also,' they added, 'I just wanted to check how Juno is? Where is she up to in her recovery? Has she had to do any rehabilitation with a vet at all?'

I replied: 'Thank you. She's got a fistula now on her amputation site, so she's being seen daily at the vets now for dressing changes.'

Later, I also received a message from someone I knew who had asked the dog sitter if they were available and could sit their dog. They had sent me the conversation so that I could read what they put.

The dog sitter had told them that they were available to sit their dogs but would need a deposit. Bearing in mind this was around the time they'd told the shooting director and others involved with the TV program that they were no longer going to be boarding dogs again! And the cheek of asking for a deposit! Where did they get the idea for that from?

They then asked if they could drive as the potential client wanted to arrange a home visit, and the dog sitter replied by saying they don't drive at the moment – I didn't even think they did drive. The potential client had stated, 'I'd like to see the place where my dogs will be staying at, please. You hear such horror stories about some places.'

The dog sitter replied by saying no problem and told the potential client that they hope to move to bigger accommodation as they want to expand and take on more sits.

So, they were apparently completely ignoring what had happened with Juno – and not only were they still taking on dog sits but were planning on expanding too! What if a dog had attacked Juno under their watch? How could that go down with even more dogs?! I couldn't believe how mindless they were being.

The potential client then asked if the dog sitter had any dogs of their own, as they'd like their dog to have company whilst staying there.

The dog sitter replied with yes – two dogs and said that was another reason they only take one booking at a time. They also stated that the potential client's dog would be coming on some of the walks throughout the day and will have and receive daily updates.

So, their dog would be coming on some of their walks?

What would happen if they'd leave that person's dog at home whilst doing these other walks? The potential client has a small dog so how would a small dog keep up with a few long hour walks; it would just be too much. Were they saying that they wouldn't be giving 100% of their attention to this dog they'd meant to be sitting, when it's their job and responsibility to make sure that dog was well cared for and out of harm's way?

If it were me looking after someone else's dog, I wouldn't let them out of my sight!

After the potential client agreed and said they'll go ahead and book their holiday, the dog sitter then asks if they have anyone to walk him when they're at work. Clearly, they were trying to get more dog walking business – by asking if they had someone to walk him during the times they were at work!

They had replied that their dog comes to work with them so there was no need for someone to walk him.

They then asked the dog sitter if they needed to see any of their dog's paperwork, flea, worming, insurance docs and vaccinations.

A responsible dog sitter will ask for proof of vaccinations – or at least make sure the vaccinations are all up to date – as well as being up to date on flea and worming treatments.

They should also tell you that they are fully licensed by the local council and insured, and preferably, they should have a DBS check certificate that they can show you. The person may be fined an unlimited amount or be imprisoned for up to six months if they provide or arrange boarding for cats or dogs without a license (or if they do not follow the conditions of their license).

They had also told me that they had messages from the dog sitter only accepting cash – which I had experience with too.

Shady as!

From what I could tell, they were just out there to make as much money as possible without caring about the dogs and their owners.

Someone else had come to me and said: 'How they walk dogs in a group like they do without being able to drive, I have no idea. They must be taking other dogs onto properties belonging to other people, which is a huge no-no.'

I had also started to notice that they were advertising on all the local group pages, which made them look like they were extremely desperate. I also doubt they were declaring the income – which would explain why they would always want to be paid in cash.

Later on, that same day, the person who had asked if the dog sitter could look after their dog for a week shortly after, received another message from them saying that they are now insured but haven't got a license to board, but could do an alternative arrangement – the dog sitter had then offered to go to their house and feed and take the dog out two times a day for an hour at a time.

Needless to say, I didn't believe that they were now insured.

I didn't and couldn't believe anything they said.

DAY 33 – FRIDAY 8TH APRIL 2022.

Today was the day of the filming for the TV program.

The film crew and the presenter had arrived at around 1pm that afternoon. I was getting nervous; I'd never done anything like this before; I'd never been on TV before! I was also getting quite excited and hoped that I would do a good job.

So, when they arrived, the shooting director knocked on our door. We let them in for a quick chat about everything, before getting Juno ready and headed out the door and walked up to the nearest park to start filming.

We walked out the front door with Juno and to my surprise a well-known TV presenter stepped out of the car. It was such a strange feeling seeing someone you've seen on TV and have them turn up right outside your house.

Then, we walked up to the local park where the filming was going to take place. The presenter and I then sat on the nearest bench to us and took a seat, my partner took Juno off a bit further up the park until it was time to film her parts.

The presenter and I had a really good in-depth conversation. We talked about issues going on in the world and everything else in between. They were a real, genuine, down-to-earth person.

The whole of the filming took a good few hours, as I was nervous and messed up quite a few times, so we had to go over the same part a few times, but luckily the weather was holding up for the most part.

The presenter had told me that they'd managed to get hold of the dog sitter and they'd managed to get a statement, which was that they were very sorry, they didn't know they needed a license to board dogs and won't be boarding dogs again.

Utter lies!

Little did the TV crew and the dog sitter know, we knew that they were still out there, happily boarding dogs – and we could prove it!

After the filming was complete, we then left the park, and we said our goodbyes and I was very much looking forward to seeing the end product. Hopefully the piece will make everyone aware of the dangers of not going with a licensed boarder.

They said it could take a few weeks to edit the film and piece it up together, and that they will let us know when and what day it would be aired on TV.

I had soon after messaged everyone to say that we had just finished filming for the TV program and that Juno is now going to be famous!

DAY 64 – MONDAY 9TH MAY 2022.

Today was the day our segment was finally due to air on the TV, we were all excited to see the piece of film. I shared it all over social media and online, messaging everyone I knew to make sure and hoping that everyone would catch our scene – at least, I hoped they would. It was still so important to me for Juno's story to get out there, reaching as many people across the UK as possible – and further.

So, that evening, we gathered around the TV and watched it live as it aired, making sure all our friends and family were watching too.

I felt a little nervous as we watched the show, waiting for our part to come on, but I also felt happy that I'd gone ahead and agreed to have it filmed. I wondered if the dog sitter would be watching this – after all, it was a prime-time show in the UK, with hundreds of thousands if not millions of viewers. Even if they didn't this when it was on live, someone they knew might have been watching, I thought, and they might pass on the message.

I hoped they would watch it and would feel some kind of guilt or remorse, but honestly, I'm not sure they're capable of doing so. If they were able to experience these feelings, surely, they would have done more to help when Juno went missing? Surely, they would have apologised – *actually* apologised? Surely, they'd have done what any normal human being with a heart and conscience would have done, and do everything in their power to help us find our beloved dog?

Either way, I hoped they would watch this, or catch a glimpse at least, and would see Juno with her three legs, how skinny she still was then, and would realise what they'd done.

Soon enough, our piece came on, and – I have to admit – it was a little strange seeing myself on TV. Unexpectedly and disappointingly, my part in the film was pretty short, and they had cut a lot out, so it was all over rather quickly.

I was glad that it was sending out the message to make sure people go with a licensed, fully checked and trusted dog sitter, but unfortunately, there wasn't enough airtime for me to tell our whole story and get my entire message across, which was quite frustrating.

Still, Juno got her piece on TV – I always knew she was a star!

DAY 71 – MONDAY 16TH MAY 2022.

I hadn't heard from the licensing officer for a while so, I decided to send them an email to check what was happening and any other updates.

'Hi,' I said, 'what's happening regarding the dog sitter? We've been researching and have found out that the dog sitter has committed animal welfare offences, as they failed to notify us or the dog warden on the day Juno went missing, even though they said they had reported her missing to the dog warden. Also, a few people are saying that the bite wounds look like definite dog bites and that dogs tend to go for the head and face when attacking; it is very rare for foxes and badgers to attack, especially if Juno was huddled up like she was. They also mentioned that the wounds on her back leg looked like they had come from a bite, probably from when she started to run away from a dog – perhaps it got a hold of her leg before she fully managed to get away.

They overcharged me and others, didn't tell me when Juno ran away, and was still carrying on with their business the whole time Juno was missing. I'm thinking that there may be a possibility that someone else was looking after her and maybe they let her escape, or I'm thinking that the dog sitter lost her before on a walk before but gave up looking because they would rather be out earning money rather than helping to save a dog's life.

Everything seems a bit off and now they seem to have blocked me from everything online, although I can still see their business page.

Oddly, they have blocked me from not being able to see the posts of the dog walks from 28th February – 13th March 2022, though, which is very odd; this was around the time Juno was being sat by the dog sitter and between the times of her disappearance.

Why wouldn't they just come clean if they are hiding something instead of causing all this drama?

This needs to be investigated properly.

Thanks.'

Then I was left to wait for their reply – and I waited and waited.

I just couldn't understand why no one seemed to be able to do anything about the situation, when it was clear who the culprit was. Whether the dog sitter had lied about what happened in terms of a dog attacking Juno or not, they had still neglected a dog in their care, and they hadn't reacted in the way a professional – or any human being really – should have reacted. It was all just so suspicious – and so frustrating.

Why did no one seem to want to look into this? Why was there, apparently, nothing or such little anyone could do about this situation? It really annoyed me.

DAY 81 – THURSDAY 26TH MAY 2022.

I finally got a reply from the licensing officer on this date, 10 days after I had emailed:

'Hi, I called in to the dog sitters' property this week but there was no response. I have previously left messages for them on their phone to contact me, but I've also not had any response to these. I have looked at council records and they do show that the dog sitter did a report with our dog warden service the day after Juno had gone missing. I must make you aware that if it is found that they are not boarding dogs at the property, then I would not be able to take further action, as dog walking and sitting- if at the owner's home, which seem to be the services they are advertising on their online business page – are not activities that are regulated under the licensing function.'

Extremely annoyed at the response that they probably won't be able to do anything about the dog sitter, I quickly replied in frustration: 'But the law states they should've reported Juno missing the day or the moment she went missing, not the day after!'

We didn't report Juno missing as we had only found out that evening and didn't know if it was a 9-5 service, and the dog sitter had said they had already reported her to the council, and we trusted them.

'And WE had to get in contact with THEM to find out she was missing, so that shows they have committed animal welfare offences right there. I've also been checking their business page and they've been letting dogs walk off-lead in a field full of livestock, which is extremely irresponsible if you ask me!'

All their response was, 'As I have explained to you in my last email, if there is no evidence of animal boarding at the property, I have no powers to investigate the dog walking. If you feel the business is being run incorrectly then I advise you to contact our trading standards team, who may be able to offer you some assistance.'

It sounded to me like they either literally had no power due to the lack of evidence, or they just didn't care about Juno getting justice. Dogs need more laws as they can't speak out for themselves. Laws need to change!

'But there is evidence that Juno was boarded at the dog sitters when they had no license!' I pointed out. 'Does that not mean anything?! The dog sitter is a very sly, cowardly human being, but not very smart.'

I soon received the following: 'My investigation is still ongoing, and I fully intend to eventually speak with them to ascertain if boarding is taking place at the property.'

Why if, why not what had already happened? To me, this is kind of like someone getting away with murder!

They continued, 'would you be willing to make a statement to that effect in the future?'

'Yes,' I replied. 'I also have evidence from when I first spoke to them enquiring about their services a while ago, to ask if they could board Juno, and they had said, we don't do boarding anymore... They had just apparently started out their business – unless they'd done it before and had just moved house and maybe changed the name of the business.'

I waited for a reply for the rest of the day, but it never came. It seemed to me that the victims in these situations just because they are dogs aren't taken seriously and something must change!

DAY 115 – WEDNESDAY 29ᵀᴴ JUNE 2022.

I had emailed the licensing officer again on the 29th of June, as I still hadn't heard a single thing from them since May:

'Hi, just wondering if you have managed to get hold of the dog sitter at all, I have heard that someone else was in their property when it happened. They also told me that the dog sitter had definitely reported Juno missing straight away that day, which we now know is a lie. They also said there were council workers who had witnessed Juno run away and tried to run after her. I've got in contact with the local council to maybe see who it was that were working up that way on the day to give a statement of what they saw and heard.'

I pressed send and then, yet again, waited for a response. A response I wasn't entirely convinced would ever come – at least, not for a long, long time.

Why were they taking around a month at a time to reply? I was starting to get very frustrated now, as we were just getting nowhere, and we needed answers!

As it had now been over three months since Juno's incident, and while she was slowly healing and recovering, I wasn't able to do the same. I needed closure, I needed to know what had happened, and I needed to know that the person responsible for all of Juno's pain, hurt and psychological issues was going to be held accountable – not just for justice for Juno, but so they would never be able to hurt any other dogs ever again. I wanted to protect and fight for Juno, but I also wanted to protect and fight for all those other dogs who could be in possible danger in the presence of this person.

This was so much bigger than just me or Juno, but no authority figure seemed to care much at all.

I just couldn't let this go. I had to do something about this, and I knew it

was probably going to be a very long and painful process.
We need justice for Juno!

DAY 141 – MONDAY 25TH JULY 2022.

For almost a month there was still no progress on anything, but then the licensing officer then eventually replied to my last email, yet again another month had gone by! Again, why had it taken so long to write an email? It just didn't make any sense.

Anyway, whatever had happened, on the 25th of July I received this message:

'I have been unable to speak to them again. I have again looked at their online business page and it seems they are now only walking dogs, and as I have previously explained to you, there is no requirement for a license to conduct this activity. Our records show that Juno was reported missing to the dog warden by them on the 8th of March 2022. Going forward, I will try to contact them again in hopes to be able to speak with them.'

The frustration and anger that I was feeling as I read this reply was unreal – how could they just let the dog sitter get away with what they'd done to Juno?!

Such a coward.

I don't understand how people can get away with things like this, it just makes you want to give up on trusting new people.

DAY 185 – WEDNESDAY 7TH SEPTEMBER 2022 – 6 months since Juno went missing.

Six months had passed since the awful day Juno had gone missing. I was still looking back to that day, unable to get the images out of my mind – not to mention all the emotions and turmoil I'd felt during those terrible 10 days – and we still hadn't got any answers to what had actually happened with Juno and the dog sitter. We still hadn't gotten anywhere regarding getting any answers to what had happened with Juno that fateful day.

To this day, the frustration and anger still run deep. Not having the answers to such a huge, monumental question is something that never leaves you – not, at least, until you're able to get at least some kind of answer. Sadly, we still didn't have any.

The good news was that Juno was getting better and stronger with each day that passed. Her mobility was improving a lot, and we were able to go out for much longer walks.

Actually, I couldn't believe how well Juno was adapting to her new life – and her new body. It was as if she kept forgetting that she only had three legs now. She could still do everything she'd done before, she still seemed to enjoy her walks and playing around with our other dog, and she was still as affectionate as ever. In terms of her physical self, she seemed to be well and truly on the mend.

But, of course, it hadn't been at all easy.

Some things were obviously hard for her to do – at least in those first few months – such as learning to walk upstairs again. She could navigate stairs and staircases, but now she had to learn how to do so with her new body, in terms of doing it without falling over and without hitting or scraping her stump, which was obviously quite painful and delicate for a while after the operation. She now treats her one back leg as a tripod by positioning it in the middle to even out and distribute her body weight.

Quite honestly, I think the whole recovery process was harder for us than it was for Juno – after all, we'd never been in this situation before, and we had no idea how hard (or not) we should be pushing her to get back to her old ways. We were terrified of making her do too much too quickly, and we constantly worried that she'd fall and hurt herself. It was a very anxious time.

For instance, the first time we took her for a proper walk outside – after months of her staying in and recovering – was scary. But being the wonder dog that she is, Juno did great. We took it slowly, and she seemed to love being outside again after overcoming fear of everything outdoors. This was the first big step towards getting back to her old self, and the normality of it was good for both Juno and us as her owners.

Another big milestone was when she was able to get upstairs easily enough - after many comical attempts – that she started sleeping upstairs in the bed again every night, instead of just sleeping on the sofa downstairs, which she'd been doing since the operation. This, again, was a big step towards normality, and it just felt so good being able to keep a close eye on her throughout the night as well as in the day.

Finally, my beloved Juno was getting back to her old self and eating solid food again. She had lost a part of her body and had many battle scars, but that didn't matter to me. What mattered most was that she was happy and healthy.

As time went by and Juno continued to heal, she got more and more confident – and far more boisterous, both with us and with her old pal, our other dog. It was so good to see her bounding and bouncing around again, seeming happy and without a care in the world.

Even so, the incident had clearly affected Juno in other ways. She may have been getting used to only having three legs, which was great, but certain things made me think and lead me to believe that she still hadn't quite gotten over what had happened – and perhaps never would, at least not totally.

For one thing, she was far clingier than she'd ever been before, which made a lot of sense. She always wanted to be around me, and she hated it whenever I had to leave her; she hated being alone. Which I, of course, could understand.

I also hated leaving her, but I knew that I needed to; after all, it was for her own good. The main reason was that I never wanted to be in a position where I had to hire a dog sitter ever again if I could help it. Even if they had all the right permits and insurance, and even if they had a million five-star reviews, I would never in good conscience be able to leave her with another sitter, not after what had happened. I just couldn't do that to her – I just couldn't risk it.

So, I made sure to ease her clinginess by leaving her for just short periods at a time – gradually making those periods longer and longer – so she would be able to get used to being alone, at least for long enough that I wouldn't need to get a sitter again. With my other dog also being there with her had also helped gain her confidence of being left alone. And, slowly but surely, she did get used to it. It's all about taking baby steps, and getting the dog used to something new gradually.

The other major change in Juno's behaviour since the incident was her reaction to other dogs, especially when we were out on walks. Before, she'd been fine with dogs approaching her, but now? Now it was a completely different story.

If she saw a dog when out on a walk, she would stop and bark loudly at them – screaming, almost. It was so strange to see her like this, and I can't imagine why she would behave in this way if she hadn't had a run-in with a dog. And, more specifically, maybe the dog sitter's dog. I would really like to know the full truth. Nothing else would explain her strange new behaviours towards other dogs. Nothing else made sense.

So, those first six months after the incident and the operation were definitely hard on everyone. It was ever so hard seeing Juno like that, and it was hard seeing how she'd changed in terms of personality. It was amazing to see how far she'd come, of course, and to see just how well she'd adapted to her new circumstances, but every time she barked at a dog out of nowhere, it was a sharp, painful reminder to me that I still didn't know what happened on that fateful day.

Perhaps one day I'll finally find out the truth of what really happened. I really, really hope so.

ONE YEAR ON: TUESDAY 7TH MARCH 2023.

A year on from the traumatic event that occurred on Monday 7th March 2022, Juno is still feeling the psychological after-effects – even a year later and has physical scars and three legs.

I never heard back from the licensing officer either.

There are clearly signs that Juno had obviously been attacked, as whenever she sees any other big dog when out on walks, she starts whining, screaming and then barking at them.

I still feel excruciating bitterness towards the whole situation that could've been easily prevented; the dog sitter gets to walk away from this with no repercussions and is continuing to walk people's dogs!

In my opinion, they are very untrustworthy human beings who only care about money – not the dogs themselves.

Fortunately, Juno has physically recovered now apart from the physical scars and the missing limb – she still doesn't realise she only has three legs - she still tries to scratch her ear with her stump! She is now also super clingy these days, which is very understandable considering everything that she's been through.

We are still continuing to work on Juno's separation anxiety, as this is very hard work that needs time and patience, and her experience has definitely been a major setback. We can now leave her alone in the house with our other dog for up to a couple of hours at a time.

Also, when we occasionally walk past the area where she ran away from, Juno gets all stressed out, and I think once we walked past their house as she kept looking back at it, obviously not feeling very comfortable about being around that particular area.

What I've learned from this experience is; call the dog warden as soon as you hear your dog has gone missing, even if the dog sitter or walker tells you that they have already done so. Just for your own piece of mind.

If you are thinking of becoming a dog sitter, or even a dog walker, I urge you to spend the money on all the relevant and most important documentation; this will protect both you and your clients if anything like this was to happen to you.

If anything like this has happened, I urge you to own up to your mistakes, take the courage to admit what you have done wrong. It's better than hiding and running away from it, you'll end up the bigger person in the end. And as you can tell from reading my experience loosely based on the events that happened, nothing will happen apart from a stern telling-off and some much-needed education.

Also, don't let the dog sitter or dog walker try and blame you for their mistakes.

The law must change!

Why is it OK for an unlicensed dog sitter to get away with what they had done to poor Juno? A helpless, innocent animal with no voice.

After all this, I am now very reluctant to leave my dogs with anyone new. I have been forced now to look for another job so that I can work from home – or, at least, closer to home. Luckily, my partner's niece and nephew often come down to help look after her, but they can't do it forever...

There are still so many mysteries and unanswered questions surrounding what had happened to Juno. Did the dog attack her? Did she get hit by a train? Did the dog sitter get someone else to look after Juno that day?

I'm not sure what else they may have lied about; I just wish I knew the full truth of what happened that fateful day.

I wrote this account because I feel others can learn and I feel that situations like this could be avoided if people were to follow the correct procedures when finding a dog sitter – and you should always make sure the person looking after your dog – your baby – has all the relevant paperwork.

In making the general public aware of the dangers that can happen if these steps aren't taken, I hope this book will help people, both now and in the future. I know everyone tends to think that this could never happen to them... but that's what I thought too.

I'm ever so grateful to every single one of you who helped me, my partner, and of course Juno, and I'm especially grateful for the internet and social media, as they let us spread the message far and wide when Juno went missing, and helped raise the required funds for her life saving surgery when Juno so desperately needed it.

If the unthinkable ever happens to you and your pet, know that there are so many good people out there, ready and willing to help – and that, fortunately, these good people will always outnumber the bad.

From me, my partner, and Juno we thank each and every one of you wholeheartedly who has supported and donated since day one!

Juno, my partner and I will forever be grateful – thank you so much for reading, much love to all.

About the author.

A W Marshall is an aspiring author hoping to continue to write books that everyone can enjoy and find interest in. Reaching out to people and giving advice in many ways, as well as making people feel better by losing themselves in another world whilst reading.

Printed in Great Britain
by Amazon

23232739R00078